SPARKLES ON THE OVAL GROUND

SEKHAR RANJAN AMIN

Printed in India

IndiePress

ISBN: 978-93-6045-834-8

First Printing, 2024

IndiePress

A division of Nasadiya Technologies Private Ltd.

Koramangala, Bangalore

Karnataka-560029

http://indiepress.in/

Edited by Pooja Janhavi

Typeset by PageMajik

Book Cover designed by Keerthipriya

Publishing Consultant – Pratik Bhamare

Dedicated

To my grandmother who taught me the first lesson of cricket.

Gratitude

To Bandana, my wife, and Aryakanya, my daughter, for their continuous help and uninterrupted inspiration in materializing this book.

Contents

PREFACE

The game of cricket is famous for its unpredictable twists and unbelievable turns, for heroic deeds by its legends, for great one-time achievements by not-so-greats, for the colorful characters who have made the game more anecdotal and romantic than any other game, for the big, sporting hearts for making it 'cricket' (opposite of 'It is not cricket'). The game's antithetical roles from the most bountiful benefactor to the most ruthless depriving agent have added extra charm to its followers spreading over three centuries and raised the factual narration of matches, achievements and sometimes lack thereof to the level of fiction and folklore.

Being a humble follower of the game, I have made a tiny effort to construct a mirror through this book which reflects some performances sparkling with the luminosity of a supernova and some not so radiant but still remarkable in the firmament of cricket during the last 150-odd years. I firmly believe that Test match is not only the best form of cricket but also exposes the entire spectrum of great qualities that this amazing game possesses. A large portion of the present day cricketers, who have benefited from various shorter forms of cricket have also admitted this. Hence, it is no wonder that my emphasis in this book is on Test cricket. That does not, however, mean that shorter versions of the game are unwelcome guests in my choice of events and statistics. They are also there with full glory and excitement.

Statistics play an important part in the narration of cricket history. My doubtless view is that eager and keen statistics-loving readers will appreciate the facts and figures of the game cited throughout the book. Not many books showcase how world records in various categories have evolved to their present shape since the beginning. A number of chapters have been dedicated in this book to give this topic of progressive records the importance it deserves. Simultaneously, the progressive records of the left-handed batters have added extra shine to this segment. To add to it, facts and figures on many first time achievements in three formats of international cricket will attract the attention of those readers who are interested in the history of the game.

Anecdotes are the jewels in the crown of cricketing folklore. They exist everywhere, in every age, in every format of cricket. This book is no exception. If the statistics of this book attract chroniclers, then its anecdotes act as the centre of attraction to the general readers.

The story, the heroism, the excitement, and the sportsmanship have decorated cricket with motherly care and affection over the ages. On the other hand, poison of politics, obnoxious opportunism, and law-defying greed for mundane things have moved heaven and earth to besmirch the blemishless flannels. Ignoring the ugly facets and accepting with gratitude only the positive side of it, this book is a modest and minuscule spectrum to record 'Sparkles on the Oval Ground.' My success will be determined only by my respected and beloved readers.

Last but not the least, I express my heartiest gratitude to the IndiePress team for providing precious and timely guidance, advice, and suggestions for making this book a reality.

Records and statistics of this book have been updated up to August 5, 2024.

1: Glory and Ignominy

Vijay Hazare

Vijay Samuel Hazare was the first Indian to score a century in each innings of a Test match—116 and 145 against Australia in Adelaide in 1947–48 (the 7th Test match of his career). Chronologically, it was the 14th instance of a batter scoring century in each innings of a Test.

He was also the first Indian to be dismissed for zero in each innings of a Test—0 and 0 against England in Kanpur in 1951–52 (the 17th Test of his career). Chronologically, it was the 71st instance of a batter dismissed for a pair of ducks in Test history.

2: First Over Delight, First Over Doom

Manohar Shankar Hardikar (born on February 8, 1936 and died on February 4, 1995) was chronologically the 85th player to play Test cricket for India. In his short span as a Test cricketer (Two Test matches and only 20 days), he achieved a unique feat.

Hardikar made his Test debut against West Indies in Mumbai. On November 28, 1958 he took the wicket of Rohan Kanhai (lbw b Hardikar 66) with the third ball of his Test career. When he came in to bat the next day, he was dismissed by the very first ball he faced in Test cricket. (lbw b Roy Gilchrist 0).

3: Waited For a Tail-ender

Amar Singh

In Test cricket, India had to wait for a tail-ender, to be precise, a number nine batter (in the batting order of the innings) to record their first ever half-century. The said half-century (an innings of 51 runs) came in the second innings of India's first ever Test match on June 28, 1932 at Lord's against England and it was scored by Ladhabhai Nakum Amar Singh, the right-arm fast bowler, who represented India in seven Tests between 1932 and 1936.

In the first innings, captain Cottari Kanakaiya Nayudu was the highest scorer for India (40 runs).

In the above-mentioned innings of 51 runs, Amar Singh hit the first ever six for India in Test cricket.

4: Cricket's Most Famous Zero, But If ...

It was Saturday, August 14, 1948. Pakistan was celebrating its first anniversary of independence and India was just one day away. Don Bradman, playing the last Test of his career, was 13 days short of his 41st birthday and only 4 runs short of owning the most sensational end-of-the-career Test batting average of 100.00.

It was the first day of The Oval Test—the 303rd match in Test history and the fifth and final Test of 'The Ashes' series of 1948. Australia had already clinched victory in three of the first four Tests of the series.

There was some delay in the commencement of the match due to the wet ground. England captain N.W.D Yardley won the toss and decided to bat first, and immediately started paying the penalty for the decision. Len Hutton, the determined opener, raised a defensive wall and scored about 60% of the team's total, but England were shot out for just 52 runs off 42 overs and one ball. Hutton was dismissed last after making 30 runs off 124 balls with one four.

In reply, Australia reached 117 for no loss. England captain Yardley threw the ball to Eric Hollies, the leg-break bowler who replaced Jim Laker in this Test.

Hollies struck immediately. Opener Sydney George Barnes (61) was trapped caught behind. In came Don Bradman. At that point of time, his batting average was 101.39 (6996 runs in 79 innings with 10 times not out). The next ball from Hollies was a leg-break. Bradman went on to his back foot and played the ball hastily, perhaps playing it off the pitch without reading the bowler's hand. The next one from Hollies was a googly. Bradman lunged forward without reading the length and the turn. The stumps and the dream were shattered, history denied.

The career ends with a duck -- Bradman at The Oval,1948

BUT IF ...

1. In the 4th Test in Leeds on July 27, 1948, Don Bradman played one of the most memorable innings of Test history—173 not out. Australia were set a target of 404 runs by England for victory, a target never achieved in Test cricket till that time. Bradman and Arthur Morris added 301 runs for the second wicket, the highest fourth innings partnership for any wicket in Test. When Australia were 400–3, just a stroke away from victory, R.N. Harvey, Bradman's batting partner, faced the first ball of the 115th over of the innings from K. Cranston. Harvey hit a four, Australia achieved a historic win and Bradman remained not out on 173. Jack Finglenton, the famous cricketer-writer, in his book, 'Brightly Fades The Don' recorded, "It would have been fitting had Bradman made the winning run, but most unselfishly, he worked the strike so that Harvey could make the winning run because of the lad's great deed (112) in the first innings." Had Bradman not been so generous, he would have ended up with 100 batting average at the end of his career despite his zero at The Oval.

2. In The Oval Test, England's batting collapsed in both innings (52 and 188). The combination of England's poor performance and Australia's batting success (389) deprived Bradman of the chance to bat for the second time in the match.

If he got to play the second innings, even a small score of 4 not out would have lifted his batting average to 100, despite the duck in the first innings.

3. When Bradman came out to bat at The Oval after the fall of Barnes' wicket, he was 13 days short of 40 years of age. The weather was gloomy. The game was about 40 minutes away from the stumps. Morris, the non-striker, expected a nightwatchman to replace Barnes. But captain Bradman did not want to hide behind a nightwatchman. Had Brandman sent a nightwatchman on that fateful evening, the probability of his achieving a Test batting average of 100 on the next day would have been much greater.

5: India's First Southpaw in Test

Phiroze Edulji Palia was the first left-handed batter in Test for India. In the first Test ever played by India (vs. England at Lord's on June 27, 1932), Palia came to bat at number seven after India lost their fifth wicket (of Sorabji Colah for 22) at 160. Palia lasted up to the team's score of 188 (his wicket was the 9th one to fall in the Indian innings). However, he managed to score only one run during the period.

P.E. Palia

The first bowler ever to bowl left-handed for India in Test was also Phiroze Edulji Palia in India's first ever Test (vs. England at Lord's on June 25, 1932). In the first innings of England, Palia, with his slow left-arm orthodox spin, bowled 4 overs, took 3 maidens, conceded only 2 runs, but failed to take any wicket.

The first left-handed bowler ever to take a Test wicket for

India was Rustomji Jamshedji Dorabji Jamshedji, the slow left-arm orthodox spinner from Mumbai. On December 16, 1933 in Mumbai, Jamshedji caught the England batter Charles John Barnett off his own bowling for 33 in the first innings of the visitors.

Vinod Kambli

The first Indian left-handed batter to score a half-century in Test was C. Ramaswami (60 runs) vs. England in Manchester on July 28, 1936. R.H. Shodhan (110 runs) was the first Indian southpaw to register a Test century against Pakistan in Kolkata on December 14, 1952. It was Shodhan's debut Test. He came at number 8 and registered the hundred. Vinod Kambli was the first Indian southpaw to record a double hundred in a Test—224 runs vs. England in Mumbai on February 22, 1993.

Vinoo Mankad was the first left-handed Indian bowler to take 5 or more wickets in a Test innings. On July 22, 1946, Mankad took 5 wickets for 101 runs against England in Manchester. On February 10, 1952, Vinoo Mankad also became the first Indian bowler to take ten or more wickets in a Test when he took 12 wickets for 108 runs (8 for 55 and 4 for 53) against England in Chennai. In this match, India recorded their first victory in Test history.

6: The Poor Boy of Batting Science

He was a magnificent, match-winning bowler with his fastish leg breaks and googlies. No version of Indian Test cricket history is complete without any reference to his bowling prowess and achievement. However, he was also famous for his lack of batting ability. He is none other than B.S. Chandrasekhar (Test career: January 21, 1964 to July 16, 1979). His bowling facts and figures are well-known. Let us have a small study of his batting figures.

Chandrasekhar batted in 80 innings in 58 Test matches. Out of these 80 innings, he batted in 75 innings at number 11, 4 times at number 10, and only once at number 9. However, out of five innings in which he did not come as number 11, Chandrasekhar came in to bat as the last batter of the innings four times. In these four innings, the batters ahead of whom Chandrasekhar appeared to bat were absent hurt. Only in the second innings of the Adelaide Test against Australia on December 28, 1967, Chandrasekhar genuinely came to bat at number 10 ahead of Umesh Kulkarni, the left-arm medium pacer. However, he was out for a duck in that innings. As number 11,

Umesh Kulkarni scored two runs. As number 10 batter, Chandrasekhar scored a total of just three runs in his Test career.

In 58 Tests, Chandrasekhar took more wickets (242) than the total runs (167) he scored.

In 32 Tests at home, Chandrasekhar scored 122 runs at an average of 5.30 runs. In 26 Tests abroad, the leg spinner managed to make only 45 runs at an average of 2.50 runs.

Chandrasekhar's longest Test innings, in terms of minutes, was of 76 minutes—16 runs with three fours against England in Kolkata on January 30, 1964 (the second Test of his career).

Chandrasekhar's highest Test score was 22 runs (23 minutes, 30 balls, four 4s) against England in Birmingham on July 15, 1967. Chandrasekhar played 38 'runless' innings in his Test career, including 23 innings in which he was dismissed for duck and 15 innings in which he remained not out without scoring.

Chandrasekhar ended his Test career with a batting average of 4.07. At any point of his Test career (i.e., at the end of any Test of his 58 Test career), his best batting average was 8.00 at the end of his second Test (vs. England in Kolkata in 1963–64).

The leg-spinner took 14 Tests and 19 innings to reach the career aggregate of 50 runs (vs. England in Birmingham on July 15, 1967). He took 3 years and 175 days to achieve this 'feat.' Chandrasekhar required 28 Tests, 40 innings, and 10 years 344 days to reach the career aggregate of 100 runs (vs. West Indies in Kolkata on December 31, 1974). To reach the 'landmark' of 150 runs, the match-winning leggie needed 43 Tests, 60 innings, and 13 years 364 days—vs. England in Chennai on January 19, 1977.

B.S. Chandrasekhar batted with 20 different batters in 80 innings of his Test career. With B.S. Bedi, he formed the most number of partnerships (26) and shared the most runs (203). The highest partnership that he shared was of 51 runs for the 10th wicket with R.G. Nadkarni (43 not out) against England in Kolkata on January 30, 1964.

In his 54th Test and 77th innings (vs. West Indies in Mumbai on December 3, 1978), Chandrasekhar scored his last Test run, just one and was bowled by Vanburn Holder. In the second innings, he was not required to bat. In the next Test in Bengaluru, he remained not out without a run in the only innings he batted. In Delhi and Kanpur Tests, Chandrasekhar did not bat. Thereafter, he played only one Test, his 58th Test against England in Birmingham. On July 14, 1979 and on July 16, 1979, he played the 79th and 80th innings respectively, and in both the innings, he remained not out without opening his account. In the 54th Test, Chandrasekhar attained batting average of 4.07, and it remained the same till his last and 58th Test.

Bhagwath Chandrasekhar

In terms of time taken, B.S. Chandrasekhar holds the world record of the longest period to reach the career aggregate of 100 runs—10 years 344 days. However, in terms of Tests and innings, world cricket has seen a worse performer in the form of Chris Martin of New Zealand, with 60 Tests and 87 innings. Martin has taken 233 wickets and scored 125 runs (in 104 innings) in 71 Tests (highest 12 not out, battling average 2.36).

Chandrasekhar was dismissed 41 times in Test cricket—23 times bowled, 7 times caught by fielders, 6 times caught behind, twice leg before wicket, twice stumped out, and once run out.

A total of 27 bowlers dismissed Chandrasekhar 40 times in Test cricket. J.K. Lever of England dismissed him the most—4 times in 5 Tests.

Chandrasekhar holds the Indian record of taking most wickets in a series—35 wickets against England in 5 Tests in 1972–73. On the other hand, his highest run aggregate in a series is only 31 in 3 Tests against New Zealand in 1976–77.

Eden Gardens, Kolkata is Chandrasekhar's best batting ground. He scored 39 runs in 6 Tests (average 9.75) on that ground.

At the time of his retirement, Chandrasekhar's 23 ducks were the world record. At the time of his retirement, his 4 'pairs' (dismissed for a duck in both innings of a Test) were also world record. Similarly, Chandrashekhar's tally of 39 unbeaten innings was also world record at the time he retired.

Had he borrowed a bit of his bowling brilliance to enlighten his bat...

7: The Century of Centuries

Warren Bardsley of Australia was the first batter to score centuries in both innings of a Test match—136 runs on August 9, 1909 (first innings) and 130 runs on August 11, 1909 (second innings)—against England at The Oval. These two hundreds were chronologically the 99th and 101st hundred in Test history.

In reply to Australia's first innings of 325 runs, England were 140 for 3 after the fall of C.B. Fry's wicket. John Sharp came in as number five batter, steadied the innings, and helped England take the first innings lead. By the time he was dismissed, England were 348-7. Sharp scored 105 in 170 minutes with 11 fours. This hundred was the 100th century in Test cricket. The date was August 10, 1909 (Tuesday). This Test was the last one of John Sharp's small career of 3 Tests and 42 days.

Incidentally, it was John Sharp who dismissed Warren Bardsley for 136 in the Australian first innings.

This England-Australia Test at The Oval, which recorded 105 of John Sharp as the 100th century in Test cricket, was chronologically the 105th Test in cricket history.

8: Run Shines at Number Ten

The glory of a Test century is bestowed upon a tail-ender (in this write-up tail-enders mean the batters who batted between numbers 9 and 11 in the batting order of the innings) very very rarely. Factually speaking, only twenty batters (21 times), batted between numbers 9 and 11, are blessed with the fortune of hitting a hundred till date. And despite that, a number 10 batter was able to manage to include himself in the list of the first 9 century-makers and the first twelve centuries in Test history. He was Walter William Read of England.

It was a three-day Test match between England and Australia at The Oval played between August 11 and 13, 1884. Australia constructed the first ever 500-plus innings in Test cricket, 551 runs all out to be precise. W.L. Murdoch registered the first ever Test double century (211) and put on the first ever double century partnership for any wicket with H.J.H. Scott—207 runs for the third wicket. In response, England lost their eighth wicket of wicketkeeper Alfred Lyttelton at 181. At the other end, the southpaw opener William Henry Scotton was providing the only resistance with 53 not out. On this background, entered Walter Read as member ten.

Scotton continued to block one end with flawless defense. At the other end, Read launched a counter-attack from the word go. The result saw the birth of a world record for the 9th wicket partnership of 151 runs, a record that lasted for more than ten years and continues to be a record for England against Australia for this wicket. When the scoreboard read 332, Scotton departed after scoring 90 runs, a new world record of the highest individual innings by a left-handed batter. Read was the last man to be dismissed for 117. England were all out for 346. However, the match was ultimately drawn.

Walter Read reached hundred in only 113 minutes with just 36 scoring shots. His 117 included 20 fours, one three, 12 twos, and 10 singles, a total of 43 scoring strokes, and it came off 155 balls in 120 minutes.

This was the first century by a number 10 batter. It came in the 16th Test and within 7 years 151 days of the beginning of Test cricket. In comparison, Test cricket had to wait 17 years 275 days and 42 Tests for a century (it was a double century) by a number 6 batter, S.E. Gregory (201) for Australia against England in Sydney on December 15, 1894.

First number seven batter to score a Test hundred was J. Briggs (121) for England vs. Australia in Melbourne on January 2, 1885 (Test match no. 18).

Coming at number eight in the batting order, the first batter ever to reach hundred was G.J. Bonnor (128) for Australia vs. England in Sydney on March 16, 1885 (Test match number 20).

First time a number nine batter got a hundred in Test was Clem Hill (160) for Australia vs. England in Adelaide on January 14, 1908 (Test match number 98).

Test cricket is yet to see a century by a number eleven batter, the highest being 98 on Test debut by A.C. Agar of Australia vs. England in Nottingham on July 11, 2013.

Walter Read

Walter Read's 117 still stands as world record by a number 10 batter in Test. On his way to this world record, he broke the previous one of 33 runs by George Alexander of Australia vs. England at The Oval in 1880.

Besides Walter Read, R.A. Duff (104) of Australia (vs. England in Melbourne on January 3, 1902), P.L.

Symcox (108) of South Africa (vs. Pakistan in Johannesburg on February 15, 1998), and Abul Hasan (113) of Bangladesh (vs. West Indies in Khulna on November 21, 2012) have hit hundreds as number 10 in the batting order.

9: Warne vs. Muralitharan: The Race for the Best

Shane Warne and Muralidharan

This story is a statistics-based narration of a thrilling race between the two contemporary champion bowlers, Shane Warne of Australia and M. Muralitharan of Sri Lanka, for reaching and then staying at the top of the wicket-taking list in Test cricket history. The story for arriving at the pinnacle of glory gained pace when one of them first broke the world record owned by the immediate predecessor, the Caribbean fast bowler Courtney Walsh.

Courtney Walsh of West Indies was the first bowler in Test cricket to bag 500 wickets. He achieved this feat in his 129th Test against South Africa in Port of Spain on March 19, 2001 (Jacques Kallis lbw b Walsh 0). Walsh finished his career with 519 wickets in 132 Tests.

M. Muralitharan of Sri Lanka broke the world record of Walsh in his 89th Test against Zimbabwe in Harare on May 8, 2004. His world record-creating 520th victim was Mluleki Nkala (caught D.P.M.D. Jayawardene bowled Muralitharan 24). However, Shane Warne, the Australian leg-break bowler, was not far behind at that point of time with 517 wickets in 110 Tests.

Muralitharan raised his world record to 527 wickets in his 90th Test on May 17, 2004 against Zimbabwe in Bulawayo. His 527th victim was Douglas Hondo (caught Attapattu bowled Muralitharan 3).

Within 57 days of Muralitharan's grabbing of world record of 527 wickets, Shane Warne rushed forward and equalled it. On July 13, 2004, in Cairns, Warne captured the 527th wicket of Upul Chandana (stumped A.C. Gilchirst bowled Warne 14) in his 112th Test. However, Warne could not surpass Murali on this occasion.

So far as Upul Chandana and Shane Warne as batters were concerned, the Cairns Test produced a rare statistical coincidence. In both the innings, Warne was out caught Thilan Samaraweera bowled Chandana (for 2 and 4 in the first and second innings respectively). Similarly, Upul Chandana was out stumped A.C. Gilchrist bowled Warne in both the innings (for 19 and 14 in the first and second innings respectively).

On August 6, 2004, against South Africa in Galle, Muralitharan broke the tie. Martin Van Jaarsveld (caught Thilan Samaraweera bowled Muralitharan 37) became the 528th victim in his 91st Test. Murali finished the Test with 532 wickets, a new world record. Boeta Dippenaar (caught D.P.M.D. Jayawardene bowled Muralitharan 11) was his 532nd wicket (taken on August 8, 2004).

But Muralitharan's stay at the top was ephemeral this time. On the second day of the India-Australia Test in Chennai (date: October 15, 2004), Shane Warne bounced back to snatch the crown from Muralitharan and picked up the 533rd wicket of his career in his 114th Test (Irfan Pathan caught Hayden bowled Warne 14). He finished the match with 537 wickets.

Shane Warne retired from Test cricket on January 5, 2007 at the end of the Sydney Test against England. His last and 708th victim was Andrew Flintoff (stumped A.C. Gilchrist bowled Warne 7). He took his last Test wicket on January 4, 2007, the 3rd day of the Sydney Test. Since October 15, 2004, Shane Warne continued his hold on the world record of most wickets for a period of 3 years and 49 days, i.e., until the 332nd day after his retirement.

A comparative study of Shane Warne's bowling figures at the time of his retirement and the Test bowling figures of Muralitharan up to the date of Shane Warne's retirement is as follows:

***

Item	**Shane Warne** (At the time of his retirement)	**M. Muralitharan** (At the time of Warne's retirement)
Tests played	145	110
Bowling innings	273	189
Balls delivered	40,705	36,705
Maiden overs	1761	1587
Runs conceded	17,995	14,649
Wickets taken	708	674
Runs conceded per wicket	25.41	21.73
Balls per wicket	57.49	54.49
Runs conceded per over	2.65	2.39
5 or more wickets in an innings	37 times	57 times
10 or more wickets in a match	10 times	19 times
Best bowling in an innings	8 wickets for 71	9 wickets for 51
Best bowling in a match	12 wickets for 128	16 wickets for 220

***

The day was Monday. The date was December 3, 2007, the third day of the Sri Lanka-England Test in Kandy. Paul Collingwood, who was batting on 45, was ready to face the 4th ball of the 33rd over from Muralitharan. England were 266 for 7. Murali bowled a well-flighted ball, good length, on the off-and-middle stump of the right-handed Collingwood. The batter misread the length and hesitated to come forward. In fact before he made a decision on his footwork, the ball clipped off the bails. A deafening roar of ecstasy that could have dwarfed the decibel generated at the time of spacecraft-launching, enveloped the stadium. **The 709th wicket! The world record. Murali's 38274th Test ball, his 116th Test and 200th bowling innings.**

Since December 3, 2007, Muralitharan has remained at the top till date.

The Last Wicket, the 800th

Muralitharan played his 132nd Test in Mumbai against India and took 4 wickets to reach 792 wickets on December 4, 2009. Sri Lanka played their next Test series against India at home. Galle was to host the first Test, which was scheduled to start on July 18, 2010. However, about a fortnight before the match, the ace right-arm off-spinner declared that he would retire from Test cricket after the Galle Test. It meant that he had only one Test left to achieve the seemingly mythological milestone of 800 wickets.

The Galle Test started half an hour late due to wet outfield. Sri Lankan captain Kumar Sangakkara won the toss and elected to bat first. With the help of centuries by opener Tharanga Paranavitana (111) and Sangakkara (103) and half-centuries by Rangana Herath (80 not out) and Lasith Malinga (64), Sri Lanka piled up 520 for 8 declared. Despite century by Virender Sehwag (109) and Yuvraj Singh's 52, India fell 244 runs short and followed on. The deadly spin of Murali earned him the wickets of Tendulkar (8), Captain M.S. Dhoni (33), Yuvraj Singh, Pragyan Ojha (3) and the debutant number 11 Abhimanyu Mithun (8). His bowling figures read 17-1-63-5. This was the world record 67th time that this legendary bowler took five or more wickets in an innings—only five bowlers (Warne 37 times, Hadlee and R Ashwin 36 times each, Kumble 35 times and Rangana Herath 34 times) achieved this feat on more than half occasions of what Murali achieved, let alone the questions of coming near to him. With this haul of 5 wickets, Murali's tally became 797.

With the commencement of the Indian second innings, the entire cricket world started praying for Murali's 800th wicket. The first four wickets of the innings were captured by the pacers. Then it was Muralitharan's turn. The combination of Mahela Jayawardene-Muralitharan dismissed Yuvraj for 5 runs, marking the 76th victim of this fielder-bowler combination. With the fall of this wicket, the fourth day's play came to an end. India at 181–5. Murali's wicket tally stood at 798.

The eighth ball of the fifth day saw Malinga capturing his fourth victim of the innings. Dhoni was out for 4 runs. India 186-6. Murali still needed two more.

The last ball of Muralitharan's 21st over was an off-spinner's wrong'un, bowled from the edge of the crease. Harbhajan Singh, the batter, attempted a sweep without bothering about the merit of the ball and the demand of the situation. He missed contact as the ball straightened and was adjudged lbw. India 197-7. Murali 799.

Mithun joined Laxman who was fighting out a losing battle. The next over was given to Malinga who was firing on all cylinders. Laxman took a single off the first ball. Somehow Mithun survived the next 2 balls off Malinga and got a single. Next over was Murali's 22nd, Mithun survived the entire over.

Laxman and Mithun provided the wall of resistance. The 24th over of Murali saw Mithun hit two fours. Two more came in the 25th over of Murali. India 219-7. When the second new ball became due, India were just two runs away from avoiding innings defeat.

Sangakkara delayed the new ball, but eventually brought back Malinga. A reverse swing and Mithun fell lbw for 25 runs off 59 balls. India's score was 246–8.

Ishant Sharma replaced Mithun. In the 86th over, Sangakkara opted for the new ball, but gave it to Murali, who conceded four runs. India 257–8.

Overs went by. Fight back of India continued. India reached 292–8 at lunch, Laxman batting 58, Ishant batting 18.

In the 38th over of Murali, Ishant played one to short third man and the batters rushed for a run that was not there. Angelo Mathews' throw defeated Laxman. He was run out for 69. India 313–9. Wicket fell in Murali's over, but he could not become the owner of it.

Ishant Sharma and Pragyan Ojha, the number 10 and 11, formed the last wicket stand. Malinga, with 5 wickets already against his name, was asked to bowl the next over. Would the batters survive to give Murali a chance?

The packed stadium prayed for Malinga's failure. And Malinga failed, despite his serious effort. So did Murali. He bowled a maiden to Ishant.

Malinga was taken off. In fear of success? Chanaka Welegedara bowled the next over. Pragyan Ojha defended solidly.

Ishant and Pragyan continued the blockade as overs passed by. Runs were coming in from here and there. The crowd was swinging from optimistic positivity to frustrating negativity. Test of patience seemed endless. Murali's 44th over ended as a maiden. India 333–9, leading by 89 runs.

Herath bowled the 115th over of the innings and conceded one run. India 334–9.

Amidst the unanswered questions of 'Will he?' and 'How long?,' Murali started his 45th over, the 116th over of the innings. Ojha defended the first ball, but lost patience facing the second one. A lofted four pushed India to 338–9. The third ball was quietly defended.

In came the fourth ball. A typical away-going delivery to left-handed Ojha who came forward. The ball took the edge. Mahela Jayawardene dived to his left at first slip and completed his 157th catch in Test.

A Vesuvius of emotion erupted in the stadium. An impossible dream touched. The 800th wicket earned. An epic career came to a fairytale-like end.

10: 99...99...99

Reaching 99 but not achieving hundred is one of the saddest stories of cricket. But fortunately this kind of misfortune does not happen as frequently as the fortune of scoring a century in any form of cricket. Still the fear of its happening remains in the minds of all passengers who journey towards the destination of century and beyond with bat in their hands.

Majid Khan

It was Sunday, March 25, 1973, the second day of the Pakistan-England Test match in Karachi. In the first innings of Pakistan, both Majid Khan (captain) and Mushtaq Mohammad, who came together to add 121 runs for the 3rd wicket, were dismissed for 99. Majid was caught by Dennis Amiss off the bowling of Pat Pocock, and Mushtaq was tragically run out. Two 99s in the same innings—no parallel instance in Test cricket. But the tragedy did not end there. England's opener Dennis Amiss became the third victim of 99 (caught Sarfraz Nawaz bowled Intikhab Alam) in this match.

As if the tragedy of being run out for 99 were not enough, Mushtaq Mohammad was dismissed for a duck in the second innings. After Pankaj Roy of India (vs. Australia in Delhi in 1959–60), Mushtaq became the second batter in Test cricket to register 99 and duck in the same match.

Mushtaq Mohammad

Sadiq Mohammad, brother of Mushtaq, and Tony Lewis, the captain of England, also came very near to hundred, 89 and 88 respectively, but could not touch the magic three-figure mark in this Test. Ultimately, the drawn Karachi Test ended without anyone hitting a hundred.

The 99s scored by Majid Khan, Mushtaq Mohammad and Dennis Amiss were chronologically the 29th, 30th, and 31st 99s in Test match history.

Although no other Test has seen three 99s till date, there are three instances of a Test match having two 99s.

Dennis Amiss

1. In 1979–80 in Perth, Kim Hughes of Australia fell victim to 99 (1st innings). It was, chronologically, the 34th ninety-nine in Test cricket. In this Test, Australia had set a tough target of 354 runs for England for victory in the fourth innings. The Australian pace duo of Geoff Dymock with 6 wickets for 34 runs and Dennis Lillee with 2 wickets for 74 runs caused the downfall of the English batters except the stubborn Yorkshireman Geoff Boycott. With his solid defensive technique and monumental patience, Boycott collected runs in ruins around him. Australians could not conquer him despite their best effort till the end of the England innings of 215. Boycott carried his bat through the innings with 99 not out (337 minutes, 285 balls, 8 fours). This was the first unbeaten innings of 99 in the history of Test cricket.

2. In 1991–92 in Christchurch, Dipak Patel was run out for 99 in the New Zealand first innings. Chronologically, he was the 9th batter (and

second New Zealander after J.E.F. Beck in 1953–54) in Test cricket to be run out for 99. After New Zealand made 312 in reply to England's first innings total of 580 for 9 declared, the touring team enforced follow on. In the New Zealand second innings, opener John Wright was playing a very responsible and defensive innings. After batting for 377 minutes, he reached 99 and stayed there for 23 minutes. Spinner Phil Tufnell tied him over after over until Wright did the wrong thing by losing his focus. He attempted a lofted shot off Tufnell and was stumped. He became only the second man in Test cricket to be stumped out for 99 after Maqsood Ahmed of Pakistan (against India in Lahore in 1954–55). Earlier, in December 1987, Wright fell victim to 99 for the first time in Test (vs. Australia in Melbourne). With this 99 in Christchurch, he became the first left-handed batter ever to achieve this luckless feat twice. Overall, Wright was chronologically the 11th left-hander to be dismissed on 99. In the only innings of England in this Christchurch Test, their star batters Robin Smith and Allan Lamb fell short of hundred by four runs and seven runs respectively.

3. In 1993 at Lord's, Australia built up a massive first innings of 632 for 4 declared. Their openers Mark Taylor and Michael Slater and number

three David Boon scored centuries. Number four Mark Waugh was well on his way to hundred, but it was that Middlesex left-arm spinner Phil Tufnell, who dismissed John Wright in Christchurch in 1991–92 for 99, came between Mark Waugh and his century and bowled him for 99. Chronologically, Mark Waugh became the 7th batter and the second Australian (after Keith Miller against England in Adelaide in 1950–51) to be dismissed bowled for 99 in Test. In the second innings of England, their opener Mike Atherton was run out for 99. He became the eighth right-handed batter to be run out for 99 in Test matches.

11: First Century

In Test Match

165 runs (retired hurt) (285 minutes, 18 fours) by C. Bannerman (Australia) vs. England in Melbourne on March 15, 1877.

For India

118 runs (185 minutes, 21 fours) by L. Amarnath vs. England in Mumbai on December 17, 1933.

Lala Amarnath

Against India

136 runs (180 minutes, 12 fours, 1 six) by B.H. Valentine (England) in Mumbai on December 17, 1933.

In One Day Internationals

103 runs (161 minutes, 134 balls, 9 fours) by D.L. Amiss (England) vs. Australia in Manchester on August 24, 1972.

For India

175 not out (138 balls, 16 fours, 6 sixes) by Kapil Dev vs. Zimbabwe at Tunbridge Wells on June 18, 1983.

Against India

137 runs (147 balls, 18 fours) by D.L. Amiss (England) at Lord's on June 7, 1975.

In T20 Internationals

117 runs (75 minutes, 57 balls, 7 fours, 10 sixes) by C.H. Gayle (West Indies) vs. South Africa in Johannesburg on September 11, 2007.

Charles Bannerman

For India

101 runs (85 minutes, 60 balls, 9 fours, 5 sixes) by S.K. Raina vs. South Africa at Gros Islet on May 2, 2010.

Against India

124 runs not out (86 minutes, 71 balls, 10 fours, 6 sixes) by S.R. Watson (Australia) in Sydney on January 31, 2016.

12: A Revolutionary and a Governor

Bina Das (born on August 24, 1911 in Krishnanagar, Bengal) was a revolutionary. She was a member of a semi-revolutionary group named "Chhatri Sangha."

Bina Das

On February 6, 1932, Bina was present in the Convocation Hall of the University of Calcutta to collect her BA (English) degree. The Governor of Bengal was the chief guest. The main purpose of Bina Das was something else. She was carrying a revolver acquired from Kamala Dasgupta, a friend of her sister Kalyani Das.

The programme started on time. When the Governor walked towards his seat, Bina got up from her chair and approached a teacher for a glass of water. However, she was asked to wait until the Governor completed his speech. As the Governor started his speech, Bina suddenly took out the revolver and fired five times at him. Incidentally, all the bullets missed the target. It was reported that one of the bullets injured a senior professor present there. Within seconds, Lieutenant Colonel Hassan Suhrawardy, the Vice-Chancellor of the University, jumped into the scene and disarmed Bina. As if nothing happened, the Governor began to address the audience in no time.

The above-said Governor remained the Governor of Bengal from 1927 to 1932.

Sir Francis Stanley Jackson

The Governor, who was born on November 21, 1870, was a Test cricketer. On July 17, 1893, he made his Test debut as the 82nd cricketer of England (vs. Australia at Lord's). On that day, when he reached seven, Arthur Shrewsbury, the England opener, became the first batter in Test history to complete 1000 runs (in his 21st Test and 37th innings). The Governor scored 91 runs in his first Test innings (caught J.M. Blackham bowled C.T.B. Turner). He became the first batter in Test cricket to be dismissed in the nervous nineties on debut and the second ever in Test cricket to be dismissed exactly on 91 (A.C. Bannerman of Australia was the first).

Once the aforementioned Governor of Bengal held the world record for the first wicket partnership in Test for a period of 10 years 209 days—185 runs first wicket stand with T.W. Hayward vs. Australia at The Oval on August 14, 1899. The Governor played all his 20 Test matches at home, the world record of playing most Tests at home without playing a single one abroad.

The Governor was **Sir Francis Stanley Jackson**.

13: No 98 in Fifty Years

India started playing Test cricket on June 25, 1932 against England at Lord's. Incidentally, in the first fifty years of Test cricket, no Indian batter was either dismissed or remained not out on the individual score of 98. However, during this period four batters (C.L. Walcott of West Indies, M.J.K. Smith of England, F.M.M. Worrell of West Indies and A.I. Kallicharran of West Indies twice) were either dismissed or remained not out on the score of 98 for five times against India. India completed 50 years of Test cricket on the second day (June 25, 1982) of their 192nd Test (vs. England in Manchester). On the following day, i.e. on June 26, 1982, Geoff Miller of England recorded the sixth innings of 98 against India.

The first Indian to record an innings of 98 in Test was Kapil Dev against West Indies on April 29, 1983 in St. John's, Antigua. It was India's 205th Test and on that day, the age of India in Test cricket was 50 years 308 days. However, for the second individual Test innings of 98, whether dismissed or not out, India did not have to wait long. Just 2 years and 128 days and 35 Tests later, Dilip Vengsarkar played an innings of 98 not out in

Colombo (SSC) against Sri Lanka on September 4, 1985.

India started playing One Day Internationals (ODI) on July 13, 1974. Their first individual innings of 98 (dismissed or unbeaten) came 17 years and 98 days later, on October 19, 1991 when N.S. Sidhu scored 98 against West Indies in Sharjah. It was India's 187th match. In T20 Internationals, no Indian has scored 98 till date. India played their first T20 Internationals on December 1, 2006, vs. South Africa in Johannesburg.

14: Historic Celebration of Birthday

C.K. Nayudu

Saturday, June 25, 1932. Venue: Lord's, London. Opponent: England. The first day of India in Test as well as international cricket. Obviously the Douglas Jardine-led England team, playing their 193rd Test overall and 21st Test at Lord's, were much stronger than C.K. Nayudu's India. The result of the match also reflected that. England: 259 and 275 for 8 declared. India 189 and 187. England won by 158 runs.

Fifty-one years later. Another Saturday. Venue: Lord's London. Opponent: West Indies. Occasion: Final of the third World Cup Cricket (Prudential Cup). It was India's 48th One Day International match and seventh against West Indies.

West Indies were the world-winning team in those days. Clive Lloyd was their captain. They demolished their opponents in the previous two World Cups, but lost the very first match of this competition to India who came to play here with just one win, and that too against a weak team East Africa, in the previous two World Cups combined. In the return match at The Oval, the Caribbeans thrashed India by 66 runs. And now, in the final, Lloyd's juggernaut was ready to steamroll India once more.

Kapil Dev

Lloyd won the toss and asked India to bat first. K. Srikkanth made the highest score of 38 off 57 balls. Mohinder Amarnath faced 80 balls to score 26. Sandeep Patil did not hit a four (he hit one six though) but earned 27 runs almost at a run-a-ball rate. Despite all these, Kapil's men were all out for 183 off 54 overs and four balls. An inglorious defeat looked inevitable.

West Indies, in reply, lost their first wicket of Gordon Greenidge to a miracle breakback from Balwinder Singh Sandhu. But Desmond Haynes and Vivian Richards began to score so freely that the spectators started anticipating the number of overs the match would last. At 50 for 1, fate began to desert West Indies. Haynes and Richards departed. Larry Gomes and Lloyd both left at 66. After tea break, Faoud Bacchus was consumed by Sandhu. Jeff Dujon and Malcolm Marshall resisted, but gradually the required run rate was rising. Once Dujon (25) was bowled by Amarnath, the Caribbean hope of staging further fightback evaporated.

Precisely at 19:25 hours London time, the sweet voice of Christopher Martin Jenkins announced the most remarkable upset of the World Cup on BBC. India emerged victorious by 43 runs.

What a historic birthday celebration it was!

15: From Three to Four Hundred

(Progressive record of the highest Test innings by left-handed batters)

Brian Lara

Thomas Kendall of Australia was the first cricketer to bat left-handed in Test cricket vs. England in Melbourne (1st Test) on March 16, 1877. He was also the first left-handed batter to score a run in Test cricket vs. England in Melbourne (1st Test) on March 16, 1877. In that innings, when he was out for 3 runs (caught James Southerton bowled Alfred Shaw), Kendall became the first left-handed batter dismissed in Test history.

John Hodges (Australia) was the first left-handed batter in Test to be dismissed for a duck vs. England in Melbourne (1st Test) on March 16, 1877.

James Lillywhite of England was the first left-handed batter to hit a four in Test cricket vs. Australia in Melbourne (1st Test) on March 17, 1877.

Here is the progressive record of the highest Test innings by a left-handed batter:

- 3 runs by Thomas Kendall (Australia) vs. England in Melbourne (1st Test) in 1876–77
- 8 runs by T. Emmett (England) vs. Australia in Melbourne (1st Test) in 1876–77
- 10 runs by James Lillywhite (England) vs. Australia in Melbourne (1st Test) in 1876–77
- 17 runs not out by Thomas Kendall (Australia) vs. England in Melbourne (1st Test) 1876–77
- 48 runs by T. Emmett (England) vs. Australia in Melbourne (2nd Test) in 1876–77
- 50 runs not out by W.H. Scotton (England) vs. Australia in Melbourne in 1881–82
- 90 runs by W.H. Scotton (England) vs. Australia at The Oval in 1884

- 101 runs by J. Darling (Australia) vs. England in Sydney in 1897–98
- 178 runs by J. Darling (Australia) vs. England in Adelaide in 1897–98
- 188 runs by C. Hill (Australia) vs. England in Melbourne in 1897–98
- 191 runs by C. Hill (Australia) vs. South Africa in Sydney in 1910–11
- 193 runs not out by W. Bardsley (Australia) vs. England at Lord's in 1926
- 216 runs not out by E. Paynter (England) vs. Australia in Nottingham in 1938
- 243 runs by E. Paynter (England) vs. South Africa in Durban in 1938–39
- 365 runs not out by G.S. Sobers (West Indies) vs. Pakistan in Kingston in 1957–58
- 375 runs by B.C. Lara (West Indies) vs. England in St. John's, Antigua in 1993–94
- 380 runs by M.L. Hayden (Australia) vs. Zimbabwe in Perth in 2003–04
- 400 runs not out by B.C. Lara (West Indies) vs. England in St. John's, Antigua in 2003–04

16: From 82 to 215

(Progressive record of the highest One Day International innings by a left-hander)

Chris Gayle

82 runs by J.H. Edrich (England) vs. Australia in Melbourne on January 5, 1971.

105 runs by R.C. Fredericks (West Indies) vs. England at The Oval on September 7, 1973.

116 runs not out by D. Lloyd (England) vs. Pakistan in Nottingham on August 31, 1974.

122 runs by D.I. Gower (England) vs. New Zealand in Melbourne on January 13, 1983.

158 runs by D.I. Gower (England) vs. New Zealand in Brisbane on January 15, 1983.

169 runs by B.C. Lara (West Indies) vs. Sri Lanka in Sharjah on October 16, 1995.

188 runs not out by G. Kirsten (South Africa) vs. U.A.E. in Rawalpindi on February 16, 1996.

194 runs by Saeed Anwar (Pakistan) vs. India in Chennai on May 21, 1997.

215 runs by C.H. Gayle (West Indies) vs. Zimbabwe in Canberra on February 24, 2015.

17: From 31 to 162

(Progressive record of the highest T20 International innings by left-handers)

Hazratullah Zazai

31 runs not out by M.E.K. Hussey (Australia) vs. New Zealand in Auckland on February 17, 2005.

41 runs by M.E. Trescothick (England) vs. Australia in Southampton on June 13, 2005.

61 runs by G.C. Smith (South Africa) vs. New Zealand in Johannesburg on October 21, 2005.

89 runs not out by G.C. Smith (South Africa) vs. Australia in Johannesburg on February 24, 2006.

117 runs by C.H. Gayle (West Indies) vs. South Africa in Johannesburg on September 11, 2007.

125 runs not out by E. Lewis (West Indies) vs. India in Kingston on July 9, 2017.

162 runs not out by Hazratullah Zazai (Afghanistan) vs. Ireland in Dehradun on February 23, 2019.

18: An Unsung Hero

He began his Test career with first ball duck in each of the two first innings of his first two Tests and five runs in each of the two second innings of his first two Tests.

He finished his 2-year-67-day Test career (from December 17, 1920 to February 22, 1923) with scores of 96, 140 and 111. He is the only batter till date to hit hundred in both innings of the last match of Test career.

When he was playing his last Test innings of 111, he was so ill that 'Wisden' recorded that he ought to have been in bed rather than on the cricket field.

Chronologically, he was only the second batter in history (after Warren Bardsley of Australia) to score century in both innings of a Test. Among the English batters, he was the first to achieve this feat.

Charles Albert George Russell

His Test career that lasted for only 10 matches and 18 innings, saw him scoring 910 runs with 5 centuries and 2 half-centuries, at an impressive average of 56.87.

The man, who was born on October 7, 1887 and died on March 23, 1961, represented Essex in the English County Championship and England in Test cricket, was **Charles Albert George Russell.**

19: He Was James Southerton

Among all Test cricketers, he was the senior most because he was born earliest, on November 16, 1827 in Petworth, Sussex. He was James Southerton of England.

James Southerton holds the oldest existing world record of Test cricket. He was a member of the England team that played in the first ever Test in cricket history—vs. Australia in Melbourne March 15–19, 1977. On the day of his Test debut, Southerton was 49 years 119 days old. Thus, he became the oldest Test debutant. This record was established even before the first ball was bowled in Test cricket. The record remains unbroken till date.

Like being the first in birth, Southerton was the first in death too. On June 16, 1880, he was the first Test cricketer to die at the age of 52 years 213 days that is within 3 years 73 days of his last Test appearance vs. Australia in Melbourne (the second Test of the series) on April 4, 1877.

Southerton was basically a round-arm right-arm slow bowler and not very skilful with the bat. In first-class cricket, he bagged 1682 wickets in 286 matches at an average of 14.43. With the bat, he scored 3159 runs at an average of just 9.02 (3 fifties, highest 82).

In Test cricket, Southerton scored seven runs and took seven wickets in two Tests. In three innings that he played in Test, he scored six, one not out and zero respectively, and on all three occasions he came to bat at number 11. He was the first batter of England and the second overall to be dismissed for a duck as number 11 in the batting order.

James Southerton

As a bowler, when James Southerton finished his Test career (his last Test was chronologically only the second one in Test cricket), he was jointly the third highest wicket-taker in Test along with his teammate Allen Hill (7 wickets) behind the leaders Thomas Kendall of Australia (14 wickets), Alfred Shaw of England (8 wickets) James Lillywhite of England (8 wickets) and W.E. Midwinter of Australia (8 wickets).

Let's finish this thumbnail sketch of James Southerton with a bizarre anecdote.

The date was July 25, 1870. Venue: The Oval, London. M.C.C. were playing against Surrey, the host. Despite having a strong batting line-up, M.C.C. were reduced from 146-2 to 157-7 and then 191 all out. Southerton bowled 32 four-ball overs and was the destroyer-in-chief with 7 wickets for 68 runs. Surrey, in response, also collapsed to 51 for 7. In walked Southerton and took strike. He unleashed a power-packed square cut, but the ball found shelter in the palms of legendary W.G. Grace at point. It wasn't a catch; the ball bounced on the ground just before it was pouched by Grace. The doctor knew it. All the fielders and the bowler knew it. The umpires, James Mortlock and George Street, also knew it. But Southerton believed that he was out, caught properly by W.G. Grace. So he started walking back to the pavilion.

Several requests were made to him for his change of mind, but Southerton remained obstinate. He left the field. The confused scorers made the entry in the scorebook: J. Southerton thinking he was out 0. Later, the entry was changed and the mode of dismissal was shown as 'retired out' in the scorebook.

20: Hanif's 499 and Two Unsolved Riddles

Hanif Mohammad, the famous Pakistani opener, piled up an epic innings of 499 in the Quaid-e-Azam Trophy semi-final for Karachi against Bahawalpur in January 1959. It was the highest individual innings in first-class cricket at that time. But in that hour of glory and historic milestones, a touch of tragedy did not go unnoticed. Hanif was run out on 499.

Not much details are available about this innings. There was no radio commentary, no television coverage. Still, based on whatever is available, a couple of riddles come to the surface only to remain unsolved till date.

A Short Description of the Match

Hanif's brother and captain of Karachi, Wazir Mohammad won the toss and elected to field first. By tea time on the first day (January 8, 1959), Bahawalpur were shot out for 185 runs. Karachi ended the first day with 59 for no loss, Hanif batting 25.

The second day saw Karachi add 324 runs to their overnight score, Hanif contributed 71% of that—230 runs. He reached 255 at stumps (Unbeaten).

Saturday, January 10, 1959 was the rest day. The match recommenced on Sunday, January 11, 1959. The matting wicket at Karachi Parsi Institute Ground was giving no assistance to the Bahawalpur bowlers. Hanif reached 300, and then 400, and then Bradman's the then world record of 452, with the inevitability of the following day's sunrise. But in a hurry to complete 500 runs before the draw of stumps, Hanif lost his wicket. Karachi declared at 772–7.

The fourth day's play lasted just 41 overs. Bahawalpur managed only 108 runs in their second innings and lost the match by an innings and 479 runs.

Riddle One

Hanif was playing the last over of the third day. He looked at the scoreboard. He saw 496 runs against his name. His only source of knowing his score authentically was that scoreboard. Just two balls were left for the day. Hanif was anxious about the overnight declaration. Thus, he decided that if he had to reach the unreachable 500, he had to do it in the next two balls. He played the penultimate ball of the day through point. Abdul Aziz, the non-striker, and Hanif ran as fast as they could. The ball was not fielded cleanly. That tempted Hanif for the second run ignoring the age-old advice of not to run off a misfield. The stumps were shattered and he was still well short. Hanif was sad and might have felt, Oh! just three more runs! But within seconds, the scenario changed. The scoreboard showed Hanif's score 499 instead of 497. Was it a mistake? Hanif was furious.

It was the semi-final of the country's biggest championship, and their star batter was on the verge of making history. Approaching 500 runs... how many times had it happened before? Never.

A scoreboard is maintained by a number of officials. Why were they not cautious, not alert to every run? Did they not know the figures they displayed determined the strategy of the innings and the fate of the game? Showing Hanif's score of 496 instead of 498 was a blunder bordering crime. Had Hanif known his score of 498 before the penultimate ball was bowled...

No information is available on whether any punishment was handed out to the responsible score-handling officials maintaining the scoreboard.

How such a Himalayan blunder was allowed to happen at such a crucial time was an unsolved riddle.

Riddle Two

This riddle could have been solved by Hanif Mohammad himself, or perhaps by his elder brother, Wazir Mohammad.

Wazir Mohammad, the captain of Karachi team in this game, was a caring elder brother of Hanif. He was called 'Wisden' by his colleagues for his sound knowledge of history and records of the game.

At the end of the second day of the match, Hanif's score was 255 not out, but he was completely exhausted. It was reported that Wazir motivated his brother by telling that Bradman's the then world record of 452 was within his reach if Hanif continued to bat in the same manner on the third day. The following day was a rest day. Wazir monitored Hanif's health and gave him an olive oil massage so that his brother would not face any fitness issue on the third day. Wazir Mohammad, as Karachi captain, also deeply observed the batting power of his opponent in this match. Bahawalpur, in their first innings, lasted only 59 overs on a placid pitch on the first day.

In light of the above, Hanif's panic-driven anticipation that the last two balls of the third day's play were his last chance to reach never-happened-before-in-history 500 runs defied logic. If he could not get the remaining four runs (Hanif, at that point in time, knew his score was 496 and not 498) that day, would his affectionate brother Wazir not wait for an over or two on the last day for his quintuple century? More so because Wazir was well aware of the lasting capability of Bahawalpur batters on the final day turf and that the continuance of his team's innings until Hanif touched history would not have affected the destiny of the match.

Hanif Mohammad

This logic-defying urgency shown by Hanif Mohammad will perhaps remain an unsolved mystery of cricket forever.

21: Morning Did Not Show the Day

Twenty-four bowlers have been able to take a wicket with their first ball in Test cricket. This achievement may be considered a bright start to a promising career. Very unfortunately, the uncertain nature of the game has influenced the progress of careers of a considerable number of promising first-ball-first-wicket bowlers adversely and pushed them to the horizon of oblivion.

Only four of these twenty-four bowlers, N.M. Lyon of Australia (530 wickets in 129 Tests), K.R. Miller of Australia (170 wickets in 55 Tests), M.W. Tate of England (155 wickets in 39 Tests), and Intikhab Alam of Pakistan (125 wickets in 47 Tests), could manage more than hundred Test wickets.

Five of these bowlers, who had already concluded their careers, could not appear in any other Test after their debut- A. Coningham of Australia (one Test, two wickets), M. Henderson of New Zealand (one Test, two wickets), H.D. Smith of New Zealand (one Test, one wicket), T.F. Johnson of West Indies (one Test, three wickets), and G.C. Viljoen of South Africa (one Test, one wicket). Despite snatching a wicket with the first ball, W.M. Bradley of England played only two Tests and took six wickets. The only Indian to take a wicket with the first ball is N.M. Kulkarni. He played his first Test against Sri Lanka in Colombo in August 1997. India won the toss, batted first and declared their first innings at 537–8. In reply, Sri Lanka were 39–0. Captain Sachin Tendulkar gave the ball to debutant spinner Kulkarni for the last over of the second day. And off the first ball of Kulkarni, Marvan Atapattu lost his wicket caught behind for 26. Chronologically, Kulkarni became the 16th bowler in Test annals to achieve this feat. However, the fall of Atapattu's wicket was followed by the longest partnership (in terms of time) in Test cricket: 753 minutes and 576 runs for the second wicket between Sanath Jayasuriya (340) and Roshan Mahanama (225). In terms of runs, the 576-run stand was a world record for any wicket at that time. N.M. Kulkarni delivered 419 more balls in that innings and conceded 195 runs but failed to add any wicket to his tally. He played only three Tests and captured two wickets in his career. His second and the last Test wicket (M.L. Hayden of Australia) came off his 590th delivery in Chennai in March, 2001.

M.K.G.C.P. Lakshita of Sri Lanka took the wicket of Mohammad Ashraful of Bangladesh with his first ball (in Colombo in 2002) but managed to play only two Tests and bag five wickets in his career.

Among the bowlers who grabbed a wicket with their first Test ball, only T.P. Horan of Australia could not manage the first wicket on his Test debut. Horan made his Test debut on March 15, 1877 vs. England in Melbourne (the first match in Test history), but bowled for the first time in his 10th Test vs. England in Sydney on January 29, 1883. He took the wicket of W.W. Read with his first ball in the second innings of England. Chronologically, this was the first instance ever of a bowler taking a wicket with his first Test ball. In all, Horan took 11 wickets in 15 Tests.

A small coincidence to end with. Two instances of a bowler taking a wicket with his first ball took place in the same Test—South Africa vs. England in Johannesburg in January 1906. On January 2, 1906, A.E.E. Vogler, the South African leg-break bowler, took a wicket and a catch with his first ball in Test. Ernest George Hayes, the English batter, was caught and bowled by Vogler for 20. When Vogler came to bat in the South African first innings, he hit a four and a six, but when his score was 14, he fell victim to J.N. Crawford of England off his first ball in Test.

22: Laker vs. Mcdonald

Jim Laker

Jim Laker of Surrey and England was a phenomenal off-spinner. In 1956, he achieved the incredible feat of taking ten wickets in an innings in a first-class match twice. On May 16, 1956, Laker took ten wickets in an innings (46 overs, 18 maidens, 88 runs, 10 wickets) for Surrey against the touring Australia team at The Oval, London. Australia were all out for 259. Colin McDonald, the opener, was the top scorer with 89.

Seventy-six days later, it was Tuesday, July 31, 1956. The fourth Test of the series in Manchester. Laker again took ten wickets in the Australian second innings of 205 (51 overs 2 balls, 23 maidens, 53 runs, 10 wickets). Australian opener Colin McDonald again became the top scorer with 89. In fact, McDonald became the top scorer in all four innings of the two matches—89 and 45 against Surrey and 32 and 89 against England. In both matches, Australia were the losers.

23: Late Attendance Went Unpunished

It was an English County Championship match played between Surrey and Essex at Leyton, on May 23, 25 and 26, 1925.

On the first day, Surrey declared their first innings at 431–8 off 110 overs. Opener J.B. Hobbs was the top scorer with 129. H.A. Peach (109) was the other century-maker. Andy Sandham, the other opener who would register the first ever triple century in Test in 1930, missed hundred by 10 runs.

In reply, Essex finished the second day with a score of 333 for 7. Like Surrey's first innings, Essex openers J.B. Freeman (125) and J.A. Cutmore (56) scored century and half-century respectively.

Tuesday, the third day of the match. May 26, 1925. The match was to start at 11:00 a.m. But the Surrey team could not reach the ground. Their bus was trapped in traffic near Stratford. However, two of the Surrey players, P.G.H. Fender, the captain, and A. Jeacocke, the leading batter, reached the ground in time as they came by car.

John William Henry Tyler Douglas, the Essex captain became impatient and was not ready to wait. He conveyed it to the umpires H.R. Butt and J. Stone. The umpires had no alternative but to agree. Surrey's two players, Fender and Jeacocke, entered the field.

Although Douglas, the Essex captain, was not ready to delay the commencement of the match due to the lack of punctuality of the Surrey team, he forgot to notice that two overnight not out batters of his team, C.J.H. Treglown and R.H. Sharp, also did not turn up by that time. Seeing delay in the batters' entry, now it became the turn of Fender to remind the umpires of the laws and claim the match.

After a while, two overnight batters, Treglown and Sharp, appeared. The third day's play commenced. It was two against two: Treglown and Sharp, the batters versus Fender and Jeacocke, the bowlers. But still, those were the days when sporting spirit had not evaporated completely from the hearts and the minds of those who carried the game forward in various capacities. Perhaps the batters were initially willing to wait for the arrival of Surrey players. Only the order of their captain pushed them to the crease. They simply played out the balls bowled by Fender and Jeacocke without attempting any scoring shots.

Within 15 minutes, the bus carrying the Surrey team arrived and the game, with a serious note, began. Essex were all out for 356 and Surrey finished the drawn game with 314 for 8 in their second innings.

The third day of the match was the 50th birthday of the Essex batter Percival Albert Perrin (born on May 26, 1876). This was his 500th first-class match. It was alleged that this veteran batter managed the press so that the event of the late arrival of the Surrey players went unreported. Even the scorers didn't reflect the few overs bowled by Fender and Jeacocke without fielders. Perhaps, this was done in fear of the bad name of the game and its administrators.

Indeed, the game was the same, but the mindset of the players and administrators towards the game was a bit different from what chroniclers observe and record today.

24: A Dive Deep Into Bradman Statistics

- Sir Don Bradman represented Australia as their 124th Test cricketer.

- Bradman played his first Test innings on December 3, 1928 (Monday) in Brisbane against England. He came to bat at number 7 after the fall of the 5th wicket of Hunter Scott Thomas Laurie Hendry (Hendry's individual score was 30 and the team's score was 71 for 5). Australian captain Jack Ryder was the other batter at the wicket. However, Bradman's first Test innings was not a long one. He scored 18 runs in 33 minutes off 40 balls with 4 fours and was dismissed leg before wicket by England pacer Maurice Tate. He was out as the 6th batter of the innings with the score reading 101 for 6. Bradman's first partnership in Test was of 30 runs in 33 minutes for the 6th wicket with Jack Ryder (33). In the second innings of the match, Bradman came at number 6 and scored only one run.

- Don Bradman attained 100+ batting average in Test for the first time on August 20, 1930, during his innings of 232 runs at The Oval against England. This was the 15th innings of his ninth Test. At the end of that innings, his batting average was exactly 103.00 (1442 runs with one not out).

- Don Bradman's highest batting average at any point in his Test career was 112.29. He attained this average at the end of his 18th Test (26th innings, aggregate 2695 runs with twice not out) when he played the innings of 299 not out against South Africa in Adelaide on February 1, 1932. His batting average remained the same in the next Test also (vs. South Africa in Melbourne on February 12–15, 1932), as he remained absent hurt.

- Don Bradman's lowest batting average at any point in his Test career was 9.50 (aggregate 19 runs) at the end of the second innings of his first Test. Bradman's second-lowest batting average at any point in his Test career was 51.33 (aggregate 308 runs) at the end of the 6th innings of his 3rd Test.

- Don Bradman had 100+ batting average at any point in his Test career (i.e., at the end of any Test match in which he participated) 17 times—at the end of his 9th Test (15th innings). 13th Test (19th innings), 15th Test (22nd innings), 16th Test (23rd innings), 18th Test (26th innings), 19th Test (26th innings), 20th Test (28th innings), 21st Test (30th innings), 22nd Test (32nd innings), 39th Test (59th innings), 40th Test (61st innings), 45th Test (69th innings), 46th Test (70th innings), 47th Test (71st innings), 48th Test (73rd innings), 49th Test (75th innings) and 51st Test (79th innings).

- Don Bradman had taken 32 catches in 99 innings (the number of innings played by his opposition when Bradman was fielding) of 52 Tests. Breakup: 20 catches in 37 Tests against England, 6 catches in 5 Tests against India, 4 catches in 5 Tests against West Indies, and 2 catches in 5 Tests against South Africa. Out of these 32 catches, he took 3 catches in the first innings of the match, 10 catches in the second innings of the match, 16 catches in the third innings of the match and 3 catches in the fourth innings of the match.

- Don Bradman had dismissed 27 batters by taking catch as fielder. He had taken two catches each of M. Leyland (England), L. Hutton (England), L. Amarnath (India), L.N. Constantine (West Indies), and T.S. Worthington (England). Bradman had taken one catch each of W.R. Hammond (England), H. Verity (England), H. Sutcliffe (England), D.C.S. Compton (England), W.J. Edrich (England), G.O.B. Allen (England), H. Larwood (England), R.E.S. Wyatt (England),

E.H. Hendren (England), W. Voce (England), M.W. Tate (England), W.E. Bowes (England), H.R. Adhikari (India), I.M. Barrow (West Indies), H.C. Griffith (West Indies), Gul Mohammad (India), H.W. Taylor (South Africa), K.S. Duleepsinhji (England), G. Kishenchand (India), C.S. Nayudu (India), J.A. Young (England), and E.L. Dalton (South Africa).

- Don Bradman had taken 32 catches off the bowling of 16 bowlers: 5 times each off the bowling of C.V. Grimmett and W.J. O'Reilly, 4 times each off H. Ironmonger and E.R.H. Toshack, 3 times off the bowling of I.W.G. Johnson, and once each off the bowling of S.J. McCabe, T.W. Wall, W.A. Johnston, L.O. Fleetwood-Smith, E.L. McCormick, S.J.E. Loxton, F.A. Ward, D.D. Blackie, P.K. Lee, D.T. Ring and F.A.W. Freer.

- Don Bradman had been dismissed 70 times in 52 Tests. Break up of mode of dismissals: Caught by fielders: 29 times, Caught by wicket keepers: 10 times, Bowled: 23 times, Leg Before Wicket: 6 times, Run Out: Once, Hit Wicket: Once.

- Twenty-nine bowlers had dismissed Don Bradman 69 times in Test cricket. H. Verity, the left-arm orthodox spinner of England, dismissed Bradman on most occasions: 8 times in 17 Tests (bowled 3, caught by fielder 4, caught by wicketkeeper 1), followed by A.V. Bedser, the right-arm medium-fast bowler of England 6 times in 10 Tests (bowled 1, caught by fielder 5). Among Indian bowlers, V.S. Hazare dismissed Bradman on most occasions, twice in 5 Tests. Bradman was out hit wicket only once in Test, by L. Amarnath of India in Brisbane on December 1, 1947. Bradman was run out only once in Test vs. England in Adelaide on February 8, 1929. The throw that ran him out was from 46-year-54-day old Jack Hobbs, the ace English batter. George Duckworth, the England wicketkeeper, gave the finishing touch on receipt of the throw from Hobbs before the 20-year-165-day old youngman Bradman regained his crease.

- Don Bradman and Walter Hammond of England were arch-rivals when it came to batting in Test matches. But even as bowlers, they took wickets of each other in Test. Hammond dismissed Don Bradman thrice in 31 Tests. Only five bowlers could dismiss Bradman on more occasions. On the other hand, one of the two wickets that Bradman had taken in Test was of Walter Hammond.

- As fielder, Hammond took two catches of Bradman in 31 Tests including one catch off his own bowling (in Adelaide in 1936–37). As fielder, Bradman caught Hammond once off the bowling of W.J. O'Reilly in Melbourne in 1936–37.

- Don Bradman had taken two wickets in Test cricket:

  (1) Ivan Barrow (West Indies) lbw b Bradman 27 (in Adelaide on December 15, 1930), and (2) Walter Hammond (England) bowled Bradman 85 (in Adelaide on January 17, 1933). There were great similarities between the two wickets taken by Bradman. Both the wickets were taken without the help of any fielder. Both the wickets were taken in Adelaide in the second innings of the opponent, that is, in the third innings of the match. The fall of both the wickets took place in the last over of the day's play, and thus, with the fall of these two wickets, the stumps were drawn. In both the Tests, George Alfred Hele was one of the two umpires. These were Hele's 6th and 14th Tests respectively as umpire. Bradman took these wickets in his 10th Test and 21st Test respectively.

- In all, Don Bradman shared 100 runs or more in a partnership 35 times in 80 Test innings—7 times with W.M. Woodfull, followed by 5 times with A.L. Hassett. Two of these 35 partnerships were of 400 runs or more, three partnerships were between 300 and 399 runs, nine partnerships were between 200 and 299 runs, and the remaining twenty-one ranged between 100 and 199 runs.

- Don Bradman formed partnerships with 35 of his teammates in 52 Tests—the most 22 times with W.M. Woodfull, followed by 21 times with S.J. McCabe. His partnerships with W.M. Woodfull produced most runs (1850), followed by partnerships with S.J. McCabe (1326 runs).

- At the time of his retirement in August 1948, Don Bradman shared three world record partnerships in Test cricket: (1) 451 runs for the second wicket with W.H. Ponsford against England at The Oval in 1934; (2) 405 runs for the 5th wicket with S.G. Barnes against England in Sydney in 1946–47; and (3) 388 runs for the 4th wicket with W.H. Ponsford against England in Leeds in 1934. Till the time of his retirement, nine partnerships (for any wicket) of 300 or more runs were registered in Test cricket. Out of these nine, five were shared by Bradman. The 5th wicket partnership of 405 runs between S.G. Barnes and Don Bradman still remains world record in Test for this wicket. The second wicket partnership of 451 runs between W.H. Ponsford and Don Bradman still remains the highest partnership for any wicket on foreign soil in Test. The 2nd wicket partnership of 301 runs between A.R. Morris and Don Bradman (vs. England in Leeds in 1948) continues to remain the highest partnership for any wicket in the fourth innings of a Test match. The 6th wicket partnership of 346 runs between J.H.W. Fingleton and Don Bradman (vs. England in Melbourne in 1936–37) remained the world record for this wicket for 72 years and 318 days. On November 19, 2009, the record was broken by Mahela Jayawardene and Prasanna Jayawardene of Sri Lanka when they added 351 runs for the sixth wicket vs. India in Ahmedabad.

- Don Bradman's highest fourth innings score in Test is 173 not out against England in Leeds in 1948. Till date, this is the third-highest score by an Australian in the fourth innings after 189 not out of S.J. McCabe and 182 by A.R. Morris (in the same innings in which Bradman recorded 173 not out). At the time of his retirement, Bradman's 173 not out stood 5th among the highest individual scores in the fourth innings of a Test.

- Don Bradman's batting average of 73.40 in the fourth innings of a Test (he scored 734 runs in 15 innings with 5 times not out) is the third highest batting average in that innings (minimum qualification: 500 runs) after Bruce Mitchell of South Africa (Average 89.85, Aggregate 629 runs in 12 innings with 5 times not out) and J.B. Stollmeyer of West Indies (Average 86.33,

Aggregate 518 runs in 10 innings with 4 times not out). Bradman scored 3 centuries in the fourth innings of a Test.

- Don Bradman's Test career lasted for 19 years and 262 days (from November 30, 1928 to August 18, 1948). During this period, a total of 128 Tests have been played internationally. Australia played 60 of these 128 Tests and Bradman played 52 of these 60.

- Don Bradman made his Test debut in Brisbane against England on November 30, 1928. It was also the first ever Test played in Brisbane.

- Don Bradman was dropped from the Australian side after he scored only 18 and 1 in his first Test.

- Don Bradman's first duck in Test cricket came in the 21st innings of his 14th Test vs. West Indies in Sydney in 1930–31 (bowled by Herman Clarence Griffith).

- Perhaps the most discussed duck in Test history was that of Don Bradman, scored in his last Test innings on August 14, 1948—the duck that took away the glory of end-of-the-career batting average of 100 from the master run machine of Australia. Chronologically, that duck of Bradman was the 1170th duck in Test history and the 345th duck for Australia. It was the 556th duck against England by any team and the 302nd duck by the Australian batters against England in Test. This tragic zero was the 118th one at The Oval and the 45th zero for Australia against England at The Oval. This duck was, chronologically, the 69th duck by any team against England at The Oval.

- Don Bradman had captained Australia in 24 Tests, won 15, drawn 6 and lost 3 Tests. In 24 Tests as captain, he scored 3147 runs with 14 hundreds at an average of 101.51.

- Don Bradman's career involved the two heaviest defeats in Test history. (1) Australia (122 and 66) lost to England (521 and 342 for 8 declared) by 675 runs in Brisbane in 1928–29. It was Bradman's debut Test. This is the world record of the heaviest loss suffered by a team by run margin. (2) Australia (201 and 123) lost to England (903 for 7 declared) by an innings and 579 runs. This is the heaviest defeat suffered by a team by an innings margin. Bradman captained Australia in this Test. However, Bradman slipped and fractured a bone in his ankle while bowling his third over in the England innings. Hence, he could not bat in both the innings that Australia played in this Test. His teammate Jack Fingleton also tore a leg muscle during the England innings.

So Australia batted with nine men in both the innings. This was Bradman's 37th Test and his 9th Test as captain.

- Don Bradman's batting average in home Tests is 98.22 (Test 33, Run 4332, Hundred 18, Fifty 10, Duck 5). His batting average in away Test is 102.84 (Test 19, Run 2674, Hundred 11, Fifty 3, Duck 2). His highest score in Australia is 299 not out against South Africa in Adelaide in 1931–32. Bradman's highest score abroad is 334 against England in Leeds in 1934.

- Don Bradman holds the world record of the highest percentage of a team's run over a batter's Test career (minimum qualification of 20 Tests). Bradman shared 24.28% of Australia's total runs in which he played. In 52 Tests, Bradman scored 6996 runs out of Australia's aggregate of 28,810 runs. Next comes the 'Black Bradman,' George Headley of West Indies with 21.38%. He scored 2190 runs in 22 Tests out of West Indies' aggregate of 10,239 runs.

Don Bradman

- Don Bradman was never dismissed in the nervous nineties in Test. But when he completed the innings of his life (February 25, 2001), he was 92 years 182 days old.

25: A Tale of Two Tragedies

A pair of tragedies, concealed inside the petals of destiny of the semi-final and final matches of the Quaid-e-Azam Trophy in Pakistan, gradually unfolded during January 1959.

The semi-final match was played between Karachi and Bahawalpur. On the first day, Bahawalpur were all out for 185. The second and the third day witnessed Karachi constructing an edifice of innings in response. When the last over of the third day (January 11, 1959) commenced, the striker Hanif Mohammad saw the scoreboard showing 496 runs against his name. He played out the first four balls, but suddenly a wave of anxiety gripped his mind. He felt that if he could not score four more runs that evening, the historic 500 would remain beyond his reach forever. Somehow for some reason he felt that there was a considerable chance of an overnight declaration of innings. So, Hanif hit the fifth ball through point, applying considerable force. The 17-year-old non-striker Abdul Aziz ran a single. But as the ball was not picked up cleanly, Hanif called his junior partner for the second run. Abdul Aziz had no alternative but to respond. Hanif was running at the danger end and despite his lung-bursting effort, he fell short of his crease and was declared run out. Sad Hanif knew he was dismissed for 497. But hardly had he left the arena, Hanif was shocked to see his score rectified to 499 on the scoreboard. Frustrated to the core of his heart and mind, Hanif knew that history had eluded him for good.

Six days later, January 17, 1959. The final of the Quaid-e-Azam Trophy was on between Karachi and Pakistan Combined Services XI. Abdul Aziz, the 17-year-old wicketkeeper-batter of Karachi, came to the wicket after the fall of the 7th wicket at 266 runs. When the score read 270, Aziz took strike off Dildar Awan, the right-arm off-spinner of the Combined XI. The ball turned, jumped sharply and hit Aziz on the chest. It was a painful blow, but the batter somehow recovered and managed to prepare himself for facing the next ball. However, before the next ball was delivered, Abdul Aziz fell on the ground and lost his consciousness. He was rushed to the hospital, but breathed his last on the way.

The scorebook entry against his name showed 'Abdul Aziz retired hurt o' in the first innings and 'Abdul Aziz absent' in the second innings with a footnote explaining what happened.

26: India's First True Opener

India started playing Test cricket on June 25, 1932 at Lord's against England. In the first four Tests, Indian innings were opened by five batters: J.G. Navle, Naoomal Jeoomal, Syed Wazir Ali, Dilwar Hussain, and Mushtaq Ali. Together in 16 innings, they scored 325 runs at a very moderate average of 21.67.

In the second Test that India played (vs. England in Mumbai in December 1933), a 5-foot-7-inch tall, 22-year-old boy made his Test debut. He was sent at number 6 by his captain C.K. Nayudu. Although he scored 23 and 30 in that match, his straight bat, grammar-prescribed backlift, composed footwork, the art of leaving the away-going deliveries and well-timed strokes gave enough indications of the shape of things to come. He was Vijay Madhavji Merchant.

In his first three Tests (the whole 3-Test series against England in India in 1933–34), Vijay Merchant was sent at number 6. He scored only 178 runs with one fifty at an average of 29.66. He played seven more Tests, all as an opener. In twelve innings, as opener, he totalled 681 runs at an average of 56.75 with three hundreds and two fifties.

In July, 1936, Vijay Merchant and Mushtaq Ali added 203 runs for the first wicket in the second innings of the Manchester Test against England. On the second day of the match (July 27, 1936), a total of 588 runs were scored, the world record of most runs in a day's play. England, in their only innings, raced from 173-2 to 571–8 declared. Facing a huge first innings deficit of 368 runs, India opened through Merchant and Mushtaq. Runs came at a break-neck speed. At the end of the day's play, India were 190 for no loss. Merchant batting 79, Mushtaq batting 105. Mushtaq's century was the first by an Indian for India on foreign soil and the second overall in Test cricket for India. On the third day, Merchant also scored hundred. Their first wicket partnership contributed 203 runs, the first ever double century stand for any wicket for India in Test cricket.

Vijay Merchant is the only Indian batter till date to hit two hundreds in the last two innings of his Test career: (1) 128 runs vs. England at The Oval in 1946 and (2) 154 runs vs. England in Delhi in 1951–52. Merchant finished his Test career with a double century partnership in 1951–52: 211 runs for the third wicket with V.S. Hazare in Delhi against England. For India, this is the highest partnership shared by a batter (for any wicket) in his last Test innings. This 211-run stand was also the highest one for any wicket for India at that time in Test cricket. It was superseded by the 4th wicket partnership of 222 runs between V.S. Hazare and V.L. Manjrekar in Leeds against England in June 1952.

On August 19, 1946, Vijay Merchant scored 128 runs at The Oval against England. It was a new record of the highest innings by an Indian for India in Test beating the previous highest of 118 by L. Amarnath in Mumbai against England on December 17, 1933. Merchant's 128 remained the highest individual innings for India for a period of 1 year 162 days, i.e., up to January 28, 1948, when V.S. Hazare made 145 in Adelaide against Australia.

However, Vijay Merchant got back that record 3 years 280 days later on November 4, 1951 in Delhi against England for about a couple of hours only. It was the last Test of Merchant, and as already stated, he and Hazare added 211 runs for the 3rd wicket. After Merchant was out for 154, Hazare surpassed him and ultimately remained not out for 164. Vijay Merchant's 154 still remains the highest score by an Indian in his last Test innings.

In first-class cricket, Merchant scored 13,470 runs in 150 matches with 45 hundreds at an average of 71.64, the second highest among the batters who finished their career, next to the insurmountable 95.14 of Don Bradman. In Test cricket, Merchant gathered 859 runs in 10 Tests with three centuries at an average of 47.72.

While assessing the career of Vijay Merchant, one has to take into account that a precious period of six years was lost from the cricketing life of this brilliant right-handed batter due to the Second World War. Further, those were the days when cricket was played on uncovered pitches, without helmet and with much inferior protective gears. Restrictions on the bowlers were also less. On this background, the very quality of runs scored by Merchant while opening the innings makes him unarguably India's first true opener in Test.

Vijay Merchant

27: Test Century Landmarks: For and Against India

First Century

For India

118 runs (185 minutes, 21 fours) by L. Amarnath against England in Mumbai on December 17, 1933. (India's 2nd Test match)

Against India

136 runs (180 minutes, 12 fours, 1 six) by B.H. Valentine of England in Mumbai on December 17, 1933. (India's 2nd Test match)

100th Century

For India

127 runs (271 minutes, 245 balls, 20 fours) by S.M. Gavaskar against Australia in Perth on December 20, 1977. (India's 154th Test match)

Against India

143 runs (343 minutes, 16 fours, 2 sixes) by G.T. Dowling of New Zealand in Dunedin on February 15, 1968. (India's 105th Test match)

200th Century

For India

121 runs (173 minutes, 111 balls, 22 fours) by M. Azharuddin against England at Lord's on July 28, 1990. (India's 265th Test match)

Against India

194 runs (554 minutes, 368 balls, 23 fours) by C.G. Greenidge of West Indies in Kanpur on October 21, 1983. (India's 214th Test match)

300th Century

For India

176 runs (419 minutes, 298 balls, 26 fours) by S.R. Tendulkar against West Indies in Kolkata on November 2, 2002. (India's 363rd Test match)

Against India

110 not out (377 minutes, 263 balls, 15 fours, 1 six) by P.A. de Silva of Sri Lanka in Mohali on November 23, 1997. (India's 313th Test match)

400th Century

For India

104 runs (274 minutes, 227 balls, 14 fours) by R. Dravid against New Zealand in Ahmedabad on November 4, 2010. (India's 443rd Test match)

Against India

123 runs (304 minutes, 196 balls, 12 fours) by M.L. Hayden of Australia in Sydney on January 5, 2008. (India's 413th Test match)

500th Century

For India

139 runs (341 minutes, 230 balls, 10 fours) by V. Kohli against West Indies in Rajkot on October 5, 2018. (India's 528th Test match)

Against India

133 runs (303 minutes, 191 balls, 13 fours, 2 sixes) by S.P.D. Smith of Australia in Brisbane on December 19, 2014. (India's 485th Test match)

Note (1): A total of 546 centuries for India and 550 centuries against India have been recorded in 579 Tests till August 5, 2024.

Note (2): S.M. Gavaskar's 107 against West Indies in Kolkata on December 29, 1978, was India's 107th Test century for India.

Note (3): S.M. Gavaskar's 147 not out against West Indies in Georgetown on April 5, 1983, was 147th Test century for India.

Note (4): G.S. Sobers' (West Indies) 108 not out in Georgetown on March 24, 1971, was the 108th century against India in Test cricket.

28: Once They Came Out of the Backstage

Test match number 1522. The third Test match of the three-Test series between South Africa and New Zealand, held in Johannesburg. Date: December 8–12, 2000.

The earlier two Tests played in Bloemfontein and Gqeberha (previously Port Elizabeth) were won by the home team by 5 wickets and 7 wickets respectively.

Rain spoiled the first day's play. Groundsmen worked hard and made the game possible on the second day.

In front of an official attendance of 5876, Shaun Pollock, the South African captain, won the toss and invited New Zealand to bat first.

Mfuneko Ngam, the South African player, who was playing his first Test, almost got a wicket in his first over. Adam Parore, the makeshift Kiwi opener, was dropped at first slip by Daryll Cullinan. However New Zealand did not last long and were all out for 200 runs off 93 overs and 5 balls. South Africa ended the day with 18–1.

More rain ruled out any play on the third and fourth day. By that time, the match was reduced to a mere formality. But still the groundsmen moved heaven and earth to improve the ground condition. The fifth day's play resumed as scheduled. The home team, already 2–0 up in the series, did not take any initiative to make the show interesting and batted out the day with the score 261–3 off 97 overs at a run rate of only 2.69. Boeta Dippenaar recorded his first Test century (100 runs off 192 balls).

However, the most memorable event took place after the match was over. Ted Wood, the match adjudicator, gave the 'Man of the Match' award to the groundsmen, Chris Scott and his staff, something that never happened before.

29: Spirit Prevailed Over Letter

DATE: February 2, 1974, Saturday.

VENUE: Queen's Park Oval, Port of Spain.

MATCH: First Test-West Indies vs. England.

CAPTAINS: R.B. Kanhai (West Indies), M.H. Denness (England).

TOSS: West Indies won and put England in.

On a damp pitch, England were in trouble in their first innings from the very beginning. Geoff Boycott, England's most technically sound opener, all of a sudden lost calmness of his mind when his and his team's score was six and attempted hook, a shot that he rarely executed throughout his career, off a short pitch delivery from Keith Boyce. Julien caught him at the boundary line and that was the beginning of the end of the tourists in this Test. Only their tall, charismatic all-rounder Tony Greig showed some resistance with a 95-minute, 79-ball innings of 37 runs. Boyce (4 wickets for 42 runs), Bernard Julien (2 wickets for 14) and Garry Sobers (two wickets for 37 runs) were good enough to bundle England out for 131 off 55 overs. West Indies finished the first day with 14–0.

Alvin Kallicharran

On the second day, West Indies were almost following England's way. By the time they put on 147 runs, half the side including Clive Lloyd, Rohan Kanhai and Garry Sobers were resting in the hut. Left-handed number 3, Alvin Kallicharran and wicketkeeper Deryck Murray (19) added 49 runs for the sixth wicket. But the real resistance was imposed by Kallicharran-Julien's 7th wicket stand.

Kallicharran completed a brilliant hundred. West Indies extended their first innings lead beyond hundred. England captain found no clue to stop the Caribbean progress. Meanwhile the Sun was in the process of setting in the distant horizon. West Indies were 274–6. Derek Underwood was going to bowl the last ball of the day as the drama began to unfold.

Julien offered a dead defensive bat to the last ball of Underwood's over. The ball rolled on to silly point where Tony Greig was fielding. As Greig bent down to pick up the ball, Alan Knott, the English glovesman, took up the onus of flicking off the bails and uprooting the stumps assuming the play was ended for the day. Julien, accordingly, left the popping crease backwards (the length of this crease on that side is infinite) on his way to the pavilion. Kallicharran, the non-striker, was already a step or two outside his popping crease at the moment Underwood delivered the last ball. Now, watching Knott disturbing the stumps on behalf of the umpires to call it a day and Julien walking off, he also stepped further forward to carry his journey back to the pavilion. But at silly point, Tony Greig noticed that the umpire had not yet called 'time' to officially declare the end of play for the day, and thus, the ball was not yet dead. Instantaneously he reacted by throwing the stumps down at the non-striker's end. A loud appeal followed. And umpire Douglas Sang Hue had no alternative but to declare Kallicharran run out for 142.

Confusion enveloped the players, except perhaps Tony Greig. Julien and Kallicharran were shell-shocked. The crowd, noticing the umpire's raised finger, became restless. The radio commentators were attempting to analyse what happened in view of the existing laws.

Meanwhile, the players left the field. As a gesture of sportsmanship, completely unaffected by what happened in the last ball of the day, Garry Sobers drove Tony Greig to his hotel to avoid public wrath.

Apparently, there were no ill feelings between the two teams.

A meeting was convened within minutes. Mike Denness and Rohan Kanhai, the two captains, Donald Carr, the manager of the England team, Douglas Sang Hue and Ralph Godfrey Gosain, the umpires and the representatives of West Indies Cricket Board participated in the meeting. A quick and rational decision was the demand of the moment.

Tony Greig

The meeting went on for more than a couple of hours. Umpire Sang Hue defended his decision to dismiss Kallicharran. However, more flexible and rational opinions influenced the final outcome. A statement was issued to the press. It was decided that in view of the larger interest of the remaining portion of the series and the game of cricket, the appeal of Greig against Kallicharran was to be withdrawn. The statement also included an apology from Tony Greig. And the event involving the last ball of the second day left no stamp of ill-feeling on the atmosphere of the remaining part of the series.

West Indies won the match by seven wickets.

30: Tears of 199

Test cricket started on March 15, 1877. But it had to wait and wait for more than a hundred years—precisely 107 years 227 days—for hunting the first hapless victim of 199—dismissed or not out.

It was the second match of the 3-Test series between Pakistan and India in Pakistan. The first Test in Lahore was drawn. The host of the second Test, chronologically the 996th one in Test annals, was Faisalabad. The pitch was slow and too much batter-friendly. The charm of uncertain ups and unpredictable downs, the asset of the game of cricket, would inevitably remain absent.

Indian captain Sunil Gavaskar won the toss and batted first. Pitch was the batter's friend, but not the friend of a strokemaker. India piled up 500 in the first innings (only their tenth 500 or more innings in Test and the first in Pakistan) in 163 overs at a rate of 3.06 runs per over. Sandeep Patil (127) and Ravi Shastri (139) hit hundreds. In reply, Pakistan batted out the rest of the 5-day match and built up an edifice of 674 for 6 in 224 overs and five balls at a rate of 2.99 runs per over.

Mohsin Khan and Mudassar Nazar, the son of the 1st century-maker in Pakistan Test history Nazar Mohammad (124 runs vs. India in Lucknow on October 25, 1952), came to open the first innings of Pakistan. This pitch was a favourite to Mudassar Nazar, the strokeless wonder of Pakistani cricket who played seven Test innings of more than 400 minutes duration in his career. The pair put on 141 runs for the first wicket. The result, the slow but assured run-flow, the failure of the ball in beating the bat—everything was as inevitable as tomorrow's sunrise in the match. Accordingly, the second wicket stand between Mudassar Nazar and Qasim Umar went on gathering runs. Pakistan crossed 200, then 300 and then 350. The partnership completed 250. The tired, yawning crowd clapped as enthusiastically as possible.

And then, in that safe valley of certainty, in came a moment of uncertainty. Mudassar reached 199 and had already batted for 552 minutes by that time. It was an off-break from Shivlal Yadav. Mudassar's tired bat found a deadly touch of the ball. Syed Kimani made no mistake behind the stumps. Mudassar, the slowest century-hitter in Test cricket (557 minutes), became the first victim of 199 in the entire history of Test match. The date was October 28, 1984, Sunday.

Mudassar's 552-minute-long innings of 199 is the fifth longest innings by a 199 run-maker in Test cricket. The distinction of the longest 199 goes to Andy Flower of Zimbabwe in Harare against South Africa on September 11, 2001. In reply to South Africa's 600–3 declared, Zimbabwe could manage only 286 runs in the first innings including a fighting 142 by Zimbabwe's wicketkeeper-batter Andy Flower. Following on, Zimbabwe lost their ninth wicket at 344. Douglas Hondo, the number 11, joined Flower who was batting on 159. Flower and Hondo provided the final resistance and added 46 runs for the tenth wicket off 97 balls. Flower's contribution was 39 runs. Zimbabwe 390 for 9. Andre Nel, the South African pacer, bowled the fourth ball of his 15th over and Flower took a single, his 199th run. Zimbabwe 391–9. Alas! Nel's next ball found Hondo right in front of the wicket. Flower remained not out on 199 off 470 balls in 590 minutes with 24 fours and one six. Chronologically, it was the sixth innings of 199 in Test and the first instance of a batter remaining not out on 199.

K.C. Sangakkara of Sri Lanka is the only other batter to remain 199 not out in Test vs. Pakistan at Galle on June 23, 2012. In Sri Lanka's first innings, the ninth wicket of Rangana Herath fell at 455. Herath was run out when his senior partner attempted a non-existent second run in a desperate try to keep strike. Sangakkara got a single, but since Herath was run out at the bowler's end, he retained his strike. His score was 182. Nuwan Pradeep was the last man in. A four, a couple of twos and a single made the left-hander Sangakkara reach 191 and Sri Lanka 464–9. Saeed Ajmal's next over produced only one run. In the next over of captain Mohammad Hafeez, Sangakkara miscued a lofted shot to what would have been mid-off. Hafeez ran to take the catch, dived, but could not latch on to it. Aajmal bowled the 153rd over of the innings. The fifth ball of the over was swept over mid-wicket by the Sri Lankan number 3 batter for six. The scoreboard showed Sri Lanka 472–9 and Sangakkara 200. He raised his bat, hearty clap enveloped the ground... and then, within seconds the scoreboard corrected itself to display Sangakkara's score 199! Frustration gripped the left-hander. Instead of playing the last ball of the over with a soft push for a comfortable single to reach 200, Sangakkar thumped it through cover, but straight to a fielder. Pradeep, the number 11, had to face Mohammad Hafeez in the next over. The second ball of Hafeez knocked off the off-stump of Pradeep. Hapless Sangakkara remained hopelessly stranded on 199.

Only two out of fourteen 199s have come in the second innings of a team and the third innings of a match—199 by S.T. Jayasuriya (Sri Lanka) against India in Colombo (SSC) on August 12, 1997 and 199 not out by Andy Flower (Zimbabwe) against South Africa in Harare on September 11, 2001.

Steve Waugh

Till date, five left-handed batters have ended their innings on 199 (out or not out)—Matthew Elliot (Australia), S.T. Jayasuriya (Sri Lanka), A. Flower (Zimbabwe), K.C. Sangakkara (Sri Lanka) and D. Elgar (South Africa). Only Matthew Elliot (Australia), S.R. Waugh (Australia), S.P.D. Smith (Australia) and A.D. Mathews (Sri Lanka) recorded their 199s abroad.

This list includes two Indians as well. M. Azharuddin was the first Indian, and chronologically the second batter, to reach 199 and not beyond it—against Sri Lanka in Kanpur in 1986–87. K.L. Rahul is the second Indian to achieve this feat—against England in Chennai in 2016–17. Out of fourteen unfortunate 199-makers, twelve batters ended up being the highest scorers of their team's innings. Only in case of Mudassar Nazar and K.L. Rahul, Qasim Umar of Paksitan with 210 and Karun Nair of India with 303 were the teams' hightest scorers respectively.

The lowest batting order in a team's innings in which a batter batted and recorded 199 is number five. The batters to do so are M. Azharuddin, S.R. Waugh, A. Flower, and Ian Bell (England).

Till date, there are five members who belonged to 199-club, but never reached double hundred. They are Matthew Elliot, M. Azharuddin, K.L. Rahul, D. Elgar and Faf du Plessis.

One Day Internationals and T20 Internationals have not yet been cruel enough to snatch the vital 200th run from a batter in an innings.

S.R. Waugh was the only batter in Test cricket to be dismissed for 199 and to share a partnership of 199 runs, although separately. Waugh scored 199 against West Indies in Bridgetown on March 27, 1999. His innings lasted for 509 minutes and 376 balls. Twenty fours and a six decorated the innings. Nearly a year later, on March 25, 2000, in the second Test in Wellington, Michael Slater (143) and S.R. Waugh (151) added 199 runs for the fifth wicket (from 51 for 4 to 250 for 5) against New Zealand off 343 balls in 216 minutes.

Muddasar Nazar

Before Mudassar Nazar inaugurated the 199-club way back in 1984, the highest score by a batter in a Test innings below 200 runs was 198. This was achieved twice:

(1) 198 not out (340 minutes, 16 fours, no six) by A.L. Hassett (Australia) against India in Adelaide on January 24, 1948, and (2) 198 runs (340 minutes, 28 fours, no six) by G.S. Sobers (West Indies) against India in Kanpur on December 16, 1958.

31: W.G. and 93

W.G. Grace

A batter comes within seven runs of a century in any first-class match. In an average scenario he becomes a bit nervous and cautious in his attempt to achieve the three-figure mark. In some rare cases, we have seen a strokeful batter hitting lofted shots to reach the coveted landmark. But when the central character in such a scenario is W.G. Grace, you cannot predict anything, simply because he is W.G., the earliest hero of this great game.

It was that era when cricket was a sweet cocktail of folklore and reality. The summer of 1898. English County Championship was going on in full swing. Sussex were scheduled to play against Gloucestershire, W.G.'s county, in Ashley Down, Bristol in a three-day match. Incidentally, W.G.'s eldest son also played in this match. He was also named William Gilbert Grace and was known as W.G. Grace Junior.

The match commenced on August 1, 1898. W.G. opened the innings for Gloucestershire after winning the toss. When the first wicket added 38 runs, Cyril Herbert George Bland, the fast bowler of Sussex, knocked off the stumps of Grace for 14. W.G.'s son, W.G. Grace Junior could score only 4. Wickets fell at regular intervals and the home team was reduced to 163–9. However, the last wicket partnership between Reginald Rice (61) and Jack Brown (47) frustrated the Sussex bowlers and added 81 runs. Gloucestershire were all out for 244. Sussex openers C.B. Fry and W.L. Murdoch, the famous batters of world cricket, played the Gloucestershire bowlers comfortably and ended the day with the team's total of 101 for no loss. Next day, Sussex were all out for 364. Fry fell just seven runs short of hundred when he was bowled by the left-arm slow bowler William Stanley Alston Brown. Murdoch made 60. Sussex took the first innings lead of 120 runs.

On the third day, Gloucestershire lost their eighth wicket for 248 in the second innings, a lead of only 128 runs. Sussex were smelling victory.

W.G. came late at number six to bat. With the help of number 10, William Stanley Alston Brown, he raised the wall of resistance. Gloucestershire crossed 300. Sussex got frustrated. After a while, Grace looked up and saw the score 341–8. The undefeated partnership for the ninth wicket added

93 runs, Grace's own score also 93 batting. The crowd started feeling the inevitability of the 116th first-class hundred of their hero.

And then came the decision of declaration. Captain Grace allowed himself to remain stranded at 93. The entire ground was in a state of confusion. Why declaration now? Why at 93?

By that time, victory of Sussex by achieving the target of 222 runs was out of question. Time left was too short. Match ended in a draw.

The mystery unfolded after the match was over. Before this innings, the 50-year-old legend finished his innings (out or not out) at every score between zero and hundred in first-class cricket except 93. As there was no practical chance of a result except draw, captain W.G. Grace did not spare the chance of achieving a feat that was never felt an achievement at all.

32: Scott and Murdoch

Lord's, the sanctum sanctorum of cricket, witnessed its first Test on Monday, July 21, 1884—exactly seven years and 128 days after Melbourne held the first ever Test in March, 1877. The Lord's Test, chronologically the 15th match in Test history, was fought between Lord Harris led England and William L. Murdoch captained Australia.

W.L Murdoch

Murdoch won the toss and chose to bat first. But Australia lost their first wicket at zero—Percy Stanislaus McDonell bowled Edmund Peate for no score. Peate caused the landslide in the Australian innings with 6 for 85. The tourists were 160–9. But Henry James Herbert Scott, playing only his second Test, and number 11 Harry Boyle gave a tough fight and added 69 runs for the tenth wicket. This was the second fifty-plus tenth wicket stand in Test cricket (after

88 runs put on by W.L. Mordoch and W. H. Moule for Australia vs. England at The Oval in 1880).

During the Australian first innings, England had to borrow the service of the Australian captain William Murdoch as a substitute fielder. When the last wicket partnership of Scott and Boyle was causing frustration to the home team, Harris invited Allan Gibson Steel, mainly known for his batting skill and later in this Test became the first cricketer to register a hundred (148) at Lord's, to bowl.

It was the second ball of Steel's second over, the 422nd ball of the innings and the 25,411th ball in Test Cricket (In those days an over was of four balls only). Scott was to take strike on 75. An aggressive shot was attempted, but the timing was missing. The ball went up and came down into the palms of Scott's captain, Murdoch, the substitute fielder of England! The wicket, which was the 480th in Test history, went in the record book as a result of the first ever catch by a substitute fielder in Test annals, and that too of a batter of the fielder's own team.

Those were the days when the game was played with bigger heart and unquestionable integrity. Thus, Murdoch accepted the catch to finish his team's innings without hesitation. And the event left no mark of animosity or negative sentiment between Scott and Murdoch.

In the next Test at The Oval, William Lloyd Murdoch (211) and Henry James Herbert Scott (102) batted together to add 207 runs for the third wicket (for Australia against England). This was the first ever double century stand for any wicket in Test cricket and Murdoch's 211 was the first ever double century in Test annals.

33: Over and Over Again

Till the Amendment to the Cricket Code, 1884 came into effect in 1889, a bowler could bowl two overs in succession in the same innings. It happened in Test cricket also. But no exhaustive list of such events till 1889 is available. In 1889, this rule was abolished.

However, even after it was prohibited, Test cricket had recorded two instances of a bowler bowling two consecutive overs in the same innings.

(1) On July 25, 1921

It was the fourth Test in Manchester between England and Australia (July 23, 25 and 26, 1921). Rain washed out the first day's play to reduce the match to a two-day affair. July 24, 1921 was the scheduled rest day.

The match began on July 25, 1921. England captain Lord Tennyson won the toss and elected to bat first. The home team started well. Opener C.A.G. Russell, playing his fifth Test, hit the second hundred of his Test career. With 40 minutes left for the day's play, England were 341–4. Perhaps, to give his bowlers a chance to exploit the nasty little session by taking a few early Australian wickets, Lord Tennyson came out and declared the innings closed.

The above decision of declaration by Lord Tennyson was very much against the existing law. As per Law 55, amended by MCC in 1914, declaration in a two-day match was not allowed later than an hour and forty minutes before the scheduled close of play. Tennyson was late in declaring the innings by an hour.

Warwick Armstrong, the Australian captain, was aware of the declaration rules. He refused to leave the field. An argument broke out. After twenty minutes, the match restarted. The England captain withdrew the declaration.

W.W. Armstrong

The state of confusion sparked by the above sudden declaration gave birth to another transgression of law. Immediately before Tennyson declared, Armstrong bowled the last over. Now, after a twenty-minute break, it was Warwick Armstrong again who bowled the first over from the other end. This went unnoticed even to the umpires Alfred Street and John Moss. The match ended in a draw.

(2) On March 28, 1951

This was a four-day Test match in Wellington between New Zealand and England (March 24, 26, 27 and 28, 1951). Like the one in 1921, the Test saw rain washing out the first day's play. March 25, 1951 was the rest day.

The match began on March 26, 1951. Walter Hadlee, the New Zealand captain playing the last Test of his career, won the toss and opted for batting first.

The Kiwi first innings lasted for just 70 eight-ball overs. Their contribution was only 125 runs. Alex Moir's 26 runs (as number 9 batter) was the top score.

England took a vital lead of 102 runs in the first innings. Len Hutton made 57. New Zealand did not do much better in their second attempt either. Roy Tattersall, the tall right-arm off-spinner from Lancashire who had taken more wickets (58) than runs scored (50) in his sixteen Test match career, reduced the New Zealanders to 105–7. Verdun Scott (60) and

Alex Moir

Alex Moir (again 26) provided some resistance before the home team got bundled out for 189 on the fourth and last day, March 28, 1951.

England needed 88 for victory in about two hours. At tea break, they were 35 for 1. Leg spinner Alex Moir bowled the last over before tea.

After tea, it was Moir again who bowled the first over. Umpires Jock McLellan and Melville Pengelly failed to notice the error. None present on the ground objected either. Ultimately, England won the match by six wickets.

In some reports at that time, it was mentioned that the mistake was committed 'in general excitement' or due to 'uncertainty on the part of the umpires.' But no official elaboration came out.

34: Lower Orders Stood High

If the progressive records of the highest partnerships for any wicket in any form of cricket is gone through, it is no wonder that the dominance of the top order partnerships (first to fifth wicket) obviously involving top order batters can be observed. For example, the present world record of the highest partnership in Test cricket is 624 runs for the third wicket between K.C. Sangakkara (number 3 in the batting order) and D.P.M.D. Jayawardene (number 4 in the batting order) for Sri Lanka against South Africa in Colombo in 2006. Similarly, in One Day Internationals, the world record of 372 runs is held by the 2nd wicket stand between C.H. Gayle (opener) and M. N. Samuel (number 3) for West Indies against Zimbabwe in Canberra on February 24, 2015. In the T20 Internationals, the world record of the highest partnership for any wicket is held by the 1st wicket stand between Lachlan Yamamoto-Lake (opener, 134 not out) and Kendel Kadowaki-Fleming (opener, 109 not out) for Japan against Chaina in Mong Kok, Hong Kong on February 15, 2024. They put on undefeated 258 runs.

But on a number of occasions, in the early days of Test cricket, the partnerships for the 8th, 9th and 10th wicket stood among the top ten record partnerships for any wicket at that time. Here are some instances:

88 runs for the 10th wicket

W.L. Murdoch (153 not out) and W. H. Moule (34) of Australia added 88 runs for the 10th wicket against England at the Oval in 1880. It was jointly the third highest partnership for any wicket in Test at that time. Chronologically, it was the 17th 50+ stand for any wicket in Test and out of these, four belonged to the 8th, 9th and 10th wicket.

151 runs for the 9th wicket

When W.H. Scotton (90) and W.W. Read (117) added 151 runs for the 9th wicket for England against Australia at The Oval in 1884, it was the third highest partnership for any wicket up to that time in Test cricket. It was also chronologically the third partnership of 150 runs or more for any wicket in Test.

154 runs for the 8th wicket

When G.J. Bonnor (128) and S.P. Jones (40) of Australia added 154 runs for the 8th wicket against England in Sydney in 1884–85, it was the 4th highest partnership for any wicket in Test at that time. It was chronologically the 5th partnership of 150 runs or more for any wicket in Test.

154 runs for the 9th wicket

When S.E. Gregory (201) and J.M. Blackham (74) added 154 runs for the 9th wicket for Australia against England in Sydney in 1894–95, it was jointly the 8th highest partnership in Test for any wicket at that time. Chronologically, it was the 12th partnership of 150 runs or more for any wicket in Test cricket.

154 runs for the 8th wicket

When C.W. Right (71) and H.R. Bromley-Davenport (84) of England added 154 runs for the 8th wicket against South Africa in Johannesburg in 1895–96, it was jointly (with two other partnerships) the 10th highest partnership for any wicket in Test at that time. Chronologically, it was the 15th partnership of 150 runs or more for any wicket in Test cricket. Out of the first 15 partnerships of 150 runs or more for any wicket in Test cricket, four belonged to 8th and 9th wicket (26.67%).

243 runs for the 8th wicket

When debutant M.J. Hartigan (116) and C. Hill (160) of Australia added 243 runs for the 8th wicket against England in Adelaide on January 15, 1908, it created a new world record of the highest partnership for any wicket in Test beating the previous record of 221 runs for the 4th wicket between G.H.S. Trott (143) and S.E. Gregory (103) for Australia against England at Lord's in 1896. Chronologically, it was the 27th partnership of 150 runs or more and the 4th partnership of 200 runs or more for any wicket in Test.

This world record of 243 runs partnership (for any wicket) lasted for 4 years 26 days. On February 10, 1912, J.B. Hobbs (178) and W. Rhodes (179) of England registered the first ever triple century partnership for any wicket in Test. The English openers added 323 runs for the 1st wicket against Australia in Melbourne (4th Test).

35: The Over That Was Never Over

That was the 1989–90 season of Shell Trophy, the domestic first-class cricket championship in New Zealand. The season was nearing its final stage. Wellington were leading the pack with 61 points. Auckland followed them with 50 points. Canterbury and Central Districts were joint third with 48 points.

Wellington were to play their last match against Canterbury in Christchurch. The second-placed Auckland were competing with Otago at the same time. Northern Districts were to play two more matches, against Otago and Central Districts.

To win the championship, Wellington's win over Canterbury was sine qua non. That would make them reach 77 points, unless they were not penalized for poor over-rate. If Auckland won over Otago and earned 16 points and if Wellington drew with a first innings lead (Wellington would get four points in that case) or lost to Canterbury, then Auckland would conquer the Trophy with 66 points. If Auckland did not win over Otago and if Canterbury defeated Wellington, then Canterbury would lift the trophy. On this background, the match between Canterbury and Wellington commenced in Lancaster Park, Christchurch on February 18, 1990.

R. T. Latham, the Canterbury captain, won the toss, but asked Wellington to bat first. Wellington reached a moderate score of 202 mainly with the help of Robert Vance's 51. Canterbury got the first innings lead and declared the innings closed at 221–7.

On the third day, February 20, 1990, John Aiken's undefeated 156 runs pushed Wellington ahead of Canterbury by 290 runs. Captain Ervin Bruce McSweeney declared the innings at 309 for 6. Canterbury were asked to score 291 runs in 59 overs for an outright victory.

But Canterbury could not exhibit the capability of a spirited chase and were reduced to 108 for 8 wickets, a hopeless situation. It appeared that Wellington's championship celebration was only a matter of time.

Connoisseurs of cricket are aware of the fact that weather change in the 22-yard arena is as fast and unpredictable as it is in the higher echelons of the Himalayas. When Canterbury's defeat looked inevitable, Lee Germon, their wicket keeper-batter and Robert Ford, the number 10, silently started raising the wall of resistance. Overs started and finished. Runs were not the priority to the defenders. Frustration crept into the line and length of the bowlers. Runs trickled in. Smile of the fielding team faded away. With twelve balls to go, Canterbury reached 196 for 8. Wellington could not lose, but they could not win either.

As hopelessness and disappointment gripped the fielding side, the Wellington think-tank of coach John Morrison and captain McSweeney decided to adopt a desperate measure. For bowling the penultimate over of the match, ball was thrown to Robert Vance, a bowler who was never known for wicket-producing delivery.

The batters Germon and Ford watched Vance overstepping without break and lobbing full tosses at them with incredible regularity. The language of invitation for coming out of the defensive shell was loud and clear. Germon obliged. His bat-swing became more forceful, and the strokes started racing to the boundary. Arms of the umpire began aching signalling fours and sixes. But bowler Vance was untiring.

As the penultimate over of the match went on and on, the umpires P.F. Carrick and D.E.C. Mckechnie lost track of the legitimate balls amidst the tsunami of no balls.

If the umpires get confused, can the scorers be far behind? They also got carried away. The scorers failed to identify, at least for the time being, which were the legitimate deliveries and what was the score at the end of each delivery. After 22 balls were bowled, the umpires called over.

Lee Germon

McSweeney asked Evan Gray, the left-arm spinner, to bowl the last over of the match. Nobody present on the field knew exactly how far Canterbury progressed towards the target of 291 as a result of the mindless bloodbath of bowling in the previous over. It was not known whether captain McSweeney passed on the same ball to Gray that he gave to Vance. But Germon, the striker, was addicted to hitting by that time.

Gray was hit for 16 by Germon off the first four balls of the over. A single occurred off the penultimate ball. Ford had to face the last ball. To ensure his team did not lose, the tail-ender offered a dead, defensive bat to the final ball of the match.

The match was over, but not the duties of the umpires and the scorers. They frantically checked and rechecked whatever they had in record, And ultimately what they found was stranger than fiction.

The penultimate over bowled by Robert Vance had only five legitimate balls and 17 no balls. As the umpires lost count, they called 'over' one ball short. The over went as under:

1st Ball	1 run off No ball
2nd Ball	4 runs off the 1st legitimate ball
3rd Ball	No ball, 4 runs off the bat
4th Ball	No ball, 4 runs off the bat
5th Ball	No ball, 6 runs off the bat
6th Ball	No ball, 6 runs off the bat
7th Ball	No ball, 4 runs off the bat
8th Ball	No ball, 6 runs off the bat
9th Ball	No ball, 1 run off the bat
10th Ball	No ball, 4 runs off the bat
11th Ball	No ball, 1 run off the bat
12th Ball	1 run off No ball
13th Ball	No ball, 6 runs off the bat
14th Ball	No ball, 6 runs off the bat
15th Ball	No ball, 6 runs off the bat
16th Ball	No ball, 6 runs off the bat
17th Ball	No ball, 6 runs off the bat
18th Ball	No run off the 2nd legitimate ball
19th Ball	No run off the 3rd legitimate ball
20th Ball	No ball, 4 runs off the bat
21st Ball	No run off the 4th legitimate ball
22nd Ball	1 run off the 5th legitimate ball
Total:	77 runs (22 balls including 17 No balls)

The 10th and the 11th ball of the over were played by Robert Ford. He scored 5 runs. The remaining 70 runs off the bat were scored by Lee Germon (8 sixes and 5 fours). It was worth noticing that all five legitimate deliveries were played by Germon and despite hitting sixes and fours off no balls at will, he could manage only 5 runs off those five legitimate balls. Two runs came off two no balls that were left unscored off by the batters. At that time, the extra run off any no ball was not awarded to the batting side if any run was scored off the bat from that ball. Another landmark during this over went unnoticed. The four hit off the 7th ball of this over brought century to Lee Germon. When the over ended 'prematurely,' the score was 273–8.

Seventeen runs off the first five balls by Germon off Evan Gray brought the scores at level-290! Just one was needed, in the parlance of tennis, 'Game, Set and Championship Point' for Canterbury to win the Trophy. But all responsible for signalling and maintenance of scores were in dark at that point of time. Ford played out the last ball and perhaps heaved a sigh of relief thinking that they were not losing. The Morrison-McSweeney doctrine almost backfired.And that was why, at the end of the match, coach John Morrison, who was keeping track of the progress in his own manner, commented that he nearly had heart failure.

The innings of Canterbury ended with Lee Germon not out 160 in 152 minutes off 143 balls with 16 fours and 8 sixes. His partner Ford remained not out 14 in 132 minutes off 69 balls with one four.

The match ended in a draw. Four points were taken away from Wellington for slow over-rate. But fortunately, they were not penalized for violation of the spirit of cricket. So, Wellington finished with 57 points. Auckland could not manage any point from their match against Otago. Wellington won the Shell Trophy.

36: Hundredth Hundred in ODI and T20I

In ODI

C.G. Greenidge

Chronologically, C.G. Greenidge of West Indies scored the hundredth hundred in One Day Internationals (ODI). He achieved this feat against Australia in Perth on January 4, 1987, the 412th match in ODI history. Incidentally, Greenidge's score in that innings was also 100 runs (165 minutes, 119 balls, 12 fours).

The above century of Greenidge was the twenty-seventh century for West Indies in their 131st match.

The hundredth hundred by a right-handed batter in ODI cricket was scored by G.A. Gooch of England (115 runs, 136 balls, 11 fours) against India in Mumbai on November 5, 1987, the 476th

ODI match. Overall, this was the 120th century in ODI history.

The hundredth hundred by a left-handed batter in ODI cricket was scored by S.P. Fleming of New Zealand (111 not out, 183 minutes, 137 balls, 5 fours) against Australia in Napier on February 12, 1998, the 1292nd match. Overall, this was the 379th century in ODI history.

In T20I

Chronologically, Kendel Kadowaki-Fleming of Japan, scored the hundredth hundred in T20 International (T20I). He scored 114 (46 balls, 10 fours, 10 sixes) against South Korea in Sano, Japan on October 15, 2022. He reached the hundred off just 40 balls. This was the 1822nd match in T20I history.

Kadowaki-Fleming's hundred was the first one for Japan in T20I. It was Japan's 4th T20I match.

The hundredth hundred by a right-handed batter in T20I has been recorded by G.J. Maxwell (Australia) on February 11, 2024 against West Indies in Adelaide. Maxwell scored 120 not out off 55 balls in 70 minutes with 12 fours and 8 sixes. This was the 2462nd match in T20I history. Left-handed batters are far away from reaching the milestone of hundred centuries in T20I matches, as they have recorded only 42 hundreds till August 5, 2024.

37: ODI Century Landmarks: For and Against India

First Century:

For India

175 runs not out (138 balls, 16 fours, 6 sixes) by Kapil Dev against Zimbabwe in Tunbridge Wells on June 18, 1983. [India's 45th ODI]

Against India

137 runs (147 balls, 18 fours) by D.L. Amiss of England at Lord's on June 7, 1975. [India's 3rd ODI]

100th Century

For India

111 runs (177 minutes, 124 balls, 7 fours, 3 sixes) by Sourav Ganguly against Kenya in Paarl on October 24, 2001. [India's 482nd ODI]

Against India

108 runs not out (75 balls, 11 fours, 5 sixes) by M.N. Samuels of West Indies in Vijayawada on November 24, 2002. [India's 516th ODI]

200th Century

For India

128 runs not out (187 minutes, 119 balls, 12 fours, 1 six) by V. Kohli against Sri Lanka in Colombo (RPS) on July 31, 2012. [India's 808th ODI]

Against India

119 runs (98 minutes, 61 balls, 3 fours, 11 sixes) by A.B. de Villiers of South Africa in Mumbai on October 25, 2015. [India's 891st ODI]

300th Century

For India

113 runs (174 minutes, 91 balls, 11 fours, 2 sixes) by V. Kohli against Bangladesh in Chattogram on December 10, 2022. [India's 1020th ODI]

Note: A total of 319 centuries have been recorded for India and a total of 249 centuries have been recorded against India in 1057 ODIs till August 5, 2024.

38: They Saw the Both

Bob Woolmer: Hanif's 499 and Lara's 501

Bob Woolmer (born on May 14, 1948), the English Test cricketer and coach, is believed to be the only one to have witnessed Hanif Mohammad's epic world record creating innings of 499 run out (in first-class cricket) and the new world record of 501 not out by Brian Lara.

On January 11, 1959, Hanif Mohammad rewrote the world record of the highest first-class innings of 452 not out by Don Bradman by making 499. Bob Woolmer was then a ten-year-old boy who was studying in a prep school in Tonbridge. His father was working in Karachi. Woolmer came to Karachi with his father who dropped him at Karachi Parsi Institute Ground (where Hanif was batting) and left for his office. Woolmer's memory of the match was not clear. He remembered the loud atmosphere, unevenness of the ground and a fall of wicket through run out. When his father came back to the ground to pick him up, he asked what happened. Woolmer's answer was "... someone got 499, Dad."

Exactly 35 years 146 days later, on June 6, 1994, Brian Lara was playing the English County Championship match against Durham at Edgbaston. At the fag end of the day, Lara broke the record of Hanif and scored 501 not out. Woolmer was the coach of Warwickshire for whom Lara was playing. According to Woolmer, Lara was so engrossed in his innings and so single-minded in reaching the never-achieved landmark of quintuple century that, despite the proverbial uncertainty of cricket, it looked inevitable.

He Almost Did It

Mushtaq Mohammad, the famous middle-order batter of Pakistan and brother of Hanif Mohammad almost emulated Bob Woolmer. Mushtaq was in the Karachi team for whom Hanif scored 499. He made 21 in his only innings of the match. On June 6, 1994, when Lara was marching on his way to the record-smashing target, Mushtaq was working in his office in Birmingham. He received a phone call that Lara crossed 450. He rushed to the ground as fast as he could, but Lara was faster than him. By the time Mushtaq arrived at the stadium, the match was over.

Alex Davis: Lara's 375 and 501

Alex Davis, as scorer, saw two record-smashing innings of 375 and 501 not out by Brian Lara.

On April 18, 1994, Lara broke the 36-year-48-day old Test world record of 365 not out by Garry Sobers of West Indies (vs. Pakistan in Kingston on March 1, 1958). For West Indies, Lara scored 375 vs. England in St. John's, Antigua. Davis was the scorer on that England tour of West Indies. Thus he had the privilege of observing each ball Lara played in that innings.

Seven weeks later, Lara built up an edifice of 501 not out for Warwickshire against Durham. Alex Davis was the scorer of Warwickshire. He noted down every detail of that landmark innings of Brian Lara.

Graham Thorpe: Lara's 375 and 400

Brian Lara broke the world record of Sobers (365 not out) on his way to score 375 for West Indies in St. John's Antigua on April 18, 1994. Graham Thorpe, the middle-order batter, was a member of the England team in that match. Thorpe watched the entire 766-minute batting show of Lara from several fielding positions on the ground and once commented that the champion batter "kept the same pace throughout his innings." Lara's overall strike rate of that innings was 69.70. However, coming at number 6, Thorpe's only innings of the match was not impressive—9 runs off 30 balls in 54 minutes.

On October 10, 2003, Matthew Hayden of Australia erased out Lara's 375 and made 380 against Zimbabwe in Perth. But his stay on the summit was short. Exactly 185 days. On April 12, 2004, Lara regained the glory with 400 not out. As he was a member of the touring team in that match, Graham Thorpe again saw the world-record innings of Lara, while fielding. It was a four-Test series between West Indies and England. England won the first three Tests comfortably. At the time the 4th Test in St. John's, Antigua began, Lara's batting was not a picture of confidence and his captaincy was in danger. Famous fast bowler of yesteryears Andy Roberts was in charge of the pitch in the fourth Test. He tried his best to make the pitch as lifeless as possible to prevent 0–4 whitewash at home. Before the match, Thorpe, the 'Player of the Match' in the previous match in Bridgetown for his 119, remarked, "For the first time I could remember Lara's footwork became unsure and he was hopping around in discomfort."

Lara won the toss and batted first. West Indies lost Daren Ganga at 33. But morning didn't show the day. Thorpe witnessed the epic battle of Lara against his form, against the enthusiastic English bowlers, and against the circumstances off the field for the next 778 minutes—a Lara quite different from what he saw 10 years earlier. England followed on, but were able to draw the match. Thorpe made 10 and 23 not out.

Darrell Hair: Lara's 375 and 400

Darrell Bruce Hair was an Australian umpire who officiated in 78 Tests, 141 ODIs and 6 T20Is as an on-field umpire. He officiated in both the matches in which Lara created new world records of 375 and 400 not out.

From the umpire's point of view, the match in which Lara scored 400 not out was not so eventful. However, both the umpires, Darrell Hair and Steve Bucknor survived a great controversy by a stroke of sheer luck at a very crucial moment in the Test Lara made 375.

On April 18, 1994, West Indian captain Courtney Walsh won the toss and did not hesitate to bat first on a docile pitch at Antigua Recreation Ground. Lara completed the triple century, the third by a Caribbean and the 13th overall on the second day. At the end of that day, he was unbeaten 320.

Sensing something historic, on the third day, the stadium was packed to the capacity and bubbling. Electronic and print media also raised hype. The 36-year-old world record of 365 runs, owned by Sir Garry Sobers, was in danger of being relegated to the status of the second highest.

When the match started on the third morning, Lara's progress was agonizingly slow. At 347, Lara got stuck up in the bowling -fielding traffic jam for 20 minutes.

A cover drive off Andy Caddick by Lara brought him at par with Sobers' world record. In the next over Chris Lewis, perhaps being overawed by the atmosphere around, bowled a loose short ball. Lara pulled it away to history. Sobers became second and none was ahead of Lara. All hell broke loose.

But, in the process of that historic pull shot, something breath-snatching happened. Lara, while attempting the shot, went so deep inside the crease that his back foot disturbed the stump-bail set up. Jack Russell, the English glovesman noticed it. The bail on the off and middle stump went up in the air and miraculously, instead of falling on the ground, came back to its original place, although 'slightly out of its slot.'

It was not known whether the umpires watched it happen. And if the bail fell on the ground...

Anderson Cummings – Lara's 375 and 501

Anderson Cummins was a Barbadian fast bowler who represented West Indies in 5 Tests and 76 ODIs. He saw Lara's innings of 375 runs as the 12th man of his team.

Brian Lara

When Lara made 501, Cummins was his opponent, playing for Durham. The irony of fate was that during this massive innings, when Lara was on 12, he was bowled by Cummins. But Cummins overstepped. Had he not done so, world cricket would have been deprived of a memorable exhibition of batting that culminated in the only quintuple century in first-class cricket. However, overstepping of Cummins was not the only one. Six runs later, wicketkeeper Chris Scott of Durham also dropped Lara.

The world of cricket blessed them both.

Bob Simpson and Two Tied Tests

Test match has seen only two tied Tests till date: (1) Australia (505 and 232) vs. West Indies (453 and 284) in Brisbane in 1960–61 (Test match no. 498, date of tie: December 14, 1960) and (2) India (397 and 347) vs. Australia (574–7 declared and 170–5 declared) in Chennai in 1986–87 (Test match no. 1052, Date of tie: September 22, 1986).

Bob Simpson of Australia took part in both the Tests. In the 1960 tied match, he scored 92 and 0 and took 3 wickets for 43 runs off 15 overs (both innings combined). He also took the catch of Conrad Hunte, West Indian opener, in the second innings.

Bob Simpson

In the second tied match, Simpson was manager of the Australian team. He was reported to have been instrumental in persuading the Aussie captain, A.R. Border to declare at the overnight score of 170 for 5 (the fourth day).

This was a tempting declaration. India needed 348 runs for victory on the fifth day pitch. India accepted the challenge and scored 347 all out.

Bob Simpson became part of cricket history.

39: From 77 to 624

(Progressive record of the highest partnership for any wicket in Test cricket)

D.P.M.D. Jayawardene

K.C. Sangakkara

77 runs for the 4th wicket between C. Bannerman (165 retired hurt) and B.B. Cooper (15) (from 41–3 to 118-4) for Australia against England in Melbourne in 1876–77 (Test match no. 1).

88 runs for the 1st wicket between N.F.D. Thomson (41) and D.W. Gregory (43) (from 0–0 to 88–1) for Australia against England in Melbourne in 1876–77 (the 2nd Test of the series) (Test match no. 2).

91 runs for the 1st wicket between E.M. Grace (36) and W.G. Grace (152) (from 0–0 to 91–1) for England against Australia at The Oval in 1880 (Test match no. 4).

120 runs for the 2nd wicket between W.G. Grace (152) and A.P. Lucas (55) (from 91–1 to 211–2) for England against Australia at The Oval in 1880 (Test match no. 4).

137 runs for the 2nd wicket between G. Ulyett (87) and J. Selby (55) (from 5–1 to 142-2) for England against Australia in Melbourne in 1881–82 (Test match no. 5).

199 runs for the 4th wicket between A.C. Bannerman (70) and P.S. McDonnell (147) (from 16–3 to 215-4) for Australia against England in Sydney in 1881–82 (Test match no. 7).

207 runs for the 3rd wicket between W.L. Murdoch (211) and H.J.H. Scott (102) (from 158-2 to 365-3) for Australia against England at The Oval in 1884 (Test match no. 16).

210 runs for the 3rd wicket between A. Ward (93) and J.T. Brown (140) (from 28–2 to 238-3) for England against Australia in Melbourne in 1894–95 (Test match no. 46).

221 runs for the 4th wicket between G.H.S. Trott (143) and S.E. Gregory (103) (from 62–3 to 283–4) for Australia against England at Lord's in 1896 (Test match no. 50).

243 runs for the 8th wicket between M.J. Hartigan (116) and C. Hill (160) (from 180–7 to 423–8) for

Australia against England in Adelaide in 1907–08 (Test match no. 98).

323 runs for the 1st wicket between J.B. Hobbs (178) and W. Rhodes (179) (from 0–0 to 323-1) for England against Australia in Melbourne in 1911–12 (Test match no. 119).

388 runs for the 4th wicket between W.H. Ponsford (181) and D.G. Bradman (304) (from 39–3 to 427-4) for Australia against England in Leeds in 1934 (Test match no. 236).

451 runs for the 2nd wicket between W.H. Ponsford (266) and D.G. Bradman (244) (from 21–1 to 472-2) for Australia against England at The Oval in 1934 (Test match no. 237).

451 runs for the 3rd wicket between Mudassar Nazar (231) and Javed Miandad (280 not out) (from 60–2 to 511–3) for Pakistan against India in Hyderabad (Sindh) in 1982–83 (Test match no. 946).

467 runs for the 3rd wicket between A.H. Jones (186) and M.D. Crowe (299) (from 148-2 to 615-3) for New Zealand against Sri Lanka in Wellington in 1990–91 (Test match no. 1162).

576 runs for the 2nd wicket between S.T. Jayasuriya (340) and R.S. Mahanama (225) (from 39–1 to

615-2) for Sri Lanka against India in Colombo (RPS) in 1997 (Test match no. 1374).

624 runs for the 3rd wicket between K.C. Sangakkara (287) and Mahela Jayawardene (374) (from 14–2 to 638-3) for Sri Lanka against South Africa in Colombo (SSC) in 2006 (Test match no. 1810).

40: When Lord's Became The Torture Cell

Sunday, July 14, 2019. Lord's, the sanctum sanctorum of cricket, was ready to host the 12th World Cup Cricket Final. This was the fifth time Lord's was given the prestigious responsibility of staging World Cup Cricket Final.

In the semi-final, England defeated Australia by 8 wickets to reach the final for the fourth time. In another semi-final, New Zealand overpowered India by 18 runs to make their way to the final for the second time. But neither England nor New Zealand could win the Cup in the past. That means, World Cup Cricket would see a new champion this time.

New Zealand skipper K.S. Williamson won the toss and batted first. With the help of Henry Nicholls (55) and wicketkeeper-batter Tom Latham (47), the visiting team could garner 241–8 off their allotted 50 overs—a total that by no means can be termed as a winning one. The home team pacers Chris Woakes took 3 for 37 and Liam Plunkett 3 for 42.

In response, England started losing wickets at regular intervals. By the time they reached 86 in the 24th over, England lost their fourth wicket in form of their captain Eoin Morgan (9). They needed 156 runs off 161 balls for victory with six wickets in hand.

Ben Stokes

The flow of the game began to take a turn in favour of England as all-rounder Ben Stokes and wicketkeeper-batter Jos Buttler arrested the downward slide. The partnership lasted for 130 balls and put on 110 runs. Buttler fell to Lockie Ferguson, the Kiwi pacer, after scoring 59 runs off 60 balls.

The seventh wicket stand between Ben Stokes and Liam Plunkett carried the score to 218-6 at the end of the 48th over—just 24 runs away from the Cup with 12 balls in hand. And, both the batters were 'infamous' to their opponents for hard and decisive hitting.

Trent Boult

Medium pacer Neesham bowled the 49th over. The first ball produced a single to Plunkett. The second one gave Stokes another single. Twenty-two runs were needed off 10 balls. Boundary-bound strokes were the demand of the moment. Plunkett obliged and took a lofted shot, but without adjusting to the slower pace of the ball. The shot lacked timing and Boult caught him at long-off. Nine balls left. Twenty-two runs still required. Stokes crossed while the catch was being taken, and thus faced the fourth ball. Another hard hit was inevitable. The fourth delivery was of full length. Stokes swung. The shot made the ball soar, but failed to make it attain 'escape velocity.' Hence, to the horror of the English supporters, the ball started coming down for landing within the midwicket boundary rope. Trent Boult was there again. But the catch was not coming to Boult directly. He ran towards the boundary to pluck it. And he plucked it. But... but... the momentum that blessed him for reaching the catch, also cursed him by carrying his existence with the ball in his hand beyond the boundary. Boult released the ball to nearby Martin Guptill, but fractionally too late. He already touched the rope. Dead Stokes became alive with six more runs. The fifth ball donated a single to Stokes. With 16 runs to go off seven balls, new batter Jofra Archer took strike and went for a mighty six in the next ball. His bat completed the swing before the ball came. Stumps were shattered, England 227–8. Six balls and fourteen runs were separating the two teams.

England required fifteen to touch the winner's trophy.

The final over was to be bowled by Trent Boult. Ben Stokes and Ali Rashid were at the crease.

50th Over

First ball: Boult to Stokes. A perfect yorker. Stokes could do nothing more than pushing it away to short extra cover. Williamson fielded. No run. England 227–8. Fifteen runs required off five balls.

Second ball: Boult to Stokes. Everyone present was feeling pressure. Another pin-pointed yorker. Stokes dug it out straight to Williamson. No run. England 227–8. Fifteen runs needed off four balls.

Third ball: Boult to Stokes. The bowler wanted to be a yorker machine. Another yorker. Slower in pace. Slightly off target in terms of length, outside the off stump. Stokes found the ball within his comfort range, bent down on his right knee, positioned himself almost beside the ball and slogged it into the horizon over midwicket for a 73 meter-six. England 233–8. Nine runs required. Three balls left.

Fourth ball: Bolt to Stokes. A low full toss. Stokes slapped it to deep midwicket. Batters sprinted for the first run and then desperately turned for the second. Guptill raced in, picked the ball up and sensing a possible run out, threw the ball aiming at the stumps at the striker's end. Irony of fate! Stokes was in a diving mode in search of the safety of the crease, the throw kissed the bat extended by Stokes for reaching the crease and tore apart the hearts of the Kiwis. The deflection mercilessly found the no-fielder zone of the ground and rolled away for four. 'Totally inadvertent' declared Nasser Hussain from the television commentary box. Stokes apologised. Umpire Kumar Dharmasena showed six fingers of his hands to convey six runs (including an overthrow for four) for England. England 239-8. Three runs to get. Two balls left.

Fifth ball: Two mishaps cancelled out the good work of the first two balls of this over by the Kiwis. Captain approached the bowler. He wanted to upset the rhythm of Stokes. A few words of advice. Then Boult went back to the top of his run-up. Yorker once again. On the off-and-middle stump. Desperate Stokes withdrew from the line of the ball and hit it to long off. The entire New Zealand knew that Stokes would not be satisfied with a single. Santner, at long off, had no reason to fall victim to pressure as he knew the second run simply did not exist. But Stokes had no alternative. To retain the strike, he ordered Rashid to take off for the second run. The measured throw reached Trent Boult in time and Boult did the rest. Umpire

Dharmasena did not even need the help of the Third Umpire to declare Ali Rashid out. England gained one precious run, New Zealand gained one invaluable wicket. Most importantly, Ben Stokes retained the strike. England 240–9. Two runs needed. One ball left. The Final reached the final ball for the final run.

Sixth Ball: The clock struck two minutes past seven in the evening. Trent Boult started the run-up for the final ball, the 600th legitimate ball of the match. By now, Boult became a yorker-maniac. Predictably, one yorker followed another, perfect or imperfect. The sixth ball was no exception. But it was a low full toss just on or outside the leg stump of Stokes. Stokes could not get room to swing freely. He placed the ball towards long-on with the primary intention of not losing the match. The new man Mark Wood and Ben Stokes ran like racing cars. Neesham picked up the ball with ice on his mind. The batters turned for the winning run. Neesham fired in the throw to Boult. Wood fell inches short. Boult broke the stumps to keep New Zealand floating and alive. England equalized, but did not win.

Tie: New Zealand 241: England 241

Super Over was arranged to break the tie. England were to bat first. They nominated Ben Stokes and Jos Buttler for opening. On the other hand, New

Zealand gave the onus to bowl the Super Over to Trent Boult.

Boult to start from where he ended the main match. So was the case of Ben Stokes.

Super Over: England Innings

First ball: Boult to Stokes. Knuckle ball. Full length. On the off stump. Beaten by the lack of pace, Stokes hit the ball clumsily in the air over the space between Colin de Grandhomme at short third man and Ross Taylor at backward point. Grandhomne defeated Taylor in chasing the ball. Before his throw reached the wicketkeeper, the batters completed the third run. England 3 for no loss.

Second ball: Boult to Buttler. Full length. On the middle stump. Buttler could not place the ball properly and played along the ground to deep square leg. A routine single. England 4 for no loss.

Third ball: Boult to Stokes. Another full-length delivery. Stokes knelt down and swept. As he did so, the body-bend and perhaps a bit of rolling of the wrist created an angle good enough to keep the deep midwicket away. Four runs. England 8 for no loss.

Fourth ball: Boult to Stokes. Full toss. Well outside the off stump. Stokes stroked it away to backward point. Lockie Ferguson's diving save reduced the score to one run. England 9 for no loss.

Fifth ball: Boult to Buttler. Yorker. On the off stump. Buttler played it away to Henry Nicholls at sweeper cover. The stroke was a controlled one and thus took an extra nanosecond to reach the fielder who, also in his mind, settled for conceding a single. Buttler took chance and ran like a hare to complete two. England 11 for no loss.

Sixth ball: Boult to Buttler. A low full toss. Buttler swung to the left of deep square leg for four. England finished with 15 for no loss. Stokes 8 not out (3 balls), Buttler 7 not out (3 balls).

Super Over: New Zealand Innings

Target for New Zealand was 16 runs off six balls. They chose M.J. Guptill and J.D.S. Neesham to open. Jofra Archer of England was asked to counter them. Till that moment, the worst over that Jofra Archer bowled in One Day Internationals yielded 15 runs. In true sense of the term, it was anybody's game.

First ball (Wide): Archer to Neesham. A yorker, but well outside the off stump. Umpire Kumar Dharmasena declared it wide. New Zealand 1 for no loss. They needed 15 runs off six balls.

First ball (Rebowled): Archer to left-handed Neesham. Yorker once more. Neesham forced the ball to long off with controlled speed that gave the batters just enough time to run for two. New Zealand 3–0. Thirteen runs required off 5 balls.

Second ball: Archer to Neesham. For a change, it was a three-quarter length ball on the off stump, which came into the batter. Neesham shuffled back and across to his off stump and swung the ball hard and high. The ball soared over the deep mid wicket boundary for six. New Zealand 9 for no loss. Seven more runs required off four balls.

Third ball: Archer to Neesham. Good length ball. Outside the off stump. Neesham glided it away to deep midwicket. Jason Roy fumbled. The batters ran twice. New Zealand 11 for no loss. The World Cup was just a stroke away. Three balls left. Choking excitement engulfed the ground.

Fourth ball: Archer to Neesham. Good length, on the off stump. Neesham glided it to the right of deep midwicket. The throw was at the bowler's end. But before Archer broke the stumps, Guptill completed the second run. New Zealand 13 for no loss. Three runs, two balls.

Fifth ball: Archer to Neesham. A short-pitch one, the first of its kind in two Super Overs. Neesham was not ready for it. He managed a mistimed pull to what might have been short cover. Archer ran in and picked up the ball. Neesham-Guptill stole a single. New Zealand 14 for no loss. Two runs, one ball. The Holy of the holies of cricket was breathless.

Sixth ball: Once more, Lord's approached the last ball of the World Cup. It was now or never for both the teams. Guptill would be taking strike for the first time in the Super Over, might be a bit rusty. While taking stance, he committed a mistake, perhaps the most vital in his cricket career. He took stance just outside the leg stump and thus, exposed his cards, revealed his intention to the opponents about the shot he was going to take. And he did not have the luxury of having any margin of error as it was the last ball. Archer's good length ball followed Guptill. He was cramped for space, and could not effect a full, mighty bat swing on the ball. Off his pads, Guptill played it to deep midwicket, straight. Jason Roy rushed in. The batters knew that they had to depend on Roy's misfield as there was no second run in it. Desperately, they turned for the second. Glovesman Buttler rushed in front of the stumps to collect the throw. Roy did not fumble, Buttler did not fumble, Guptill dived. But the World Cup fell a yard short. Guptill run out for 1 off 1 ball. Neesham not out 13 off 5 balls. Wide 1. New

Zealand 15–1. Tie followed tie. The clock struck 07–29 in the evening.

After the Super Over was tied, as per rules of the tournament, the boundary count back rule was applied as tie-breaker. The rule is as under:

- In the event of a Super Over tie, the team that hits more boundaries (main match and Super Over combined) shall be the winner.
- If the number of boundaries hit by both teams is equal, the team whose batters scored more boundaries during its innings in the main match only shall be the winner.
- If still the tie is not broken, a count-back from the final ball of the Super Over will be conducted. The team with the higher-scoring delivery shall be the winner. If a team loses two wickets during its Super Over, then any unbowled deliveries will be counted as dot balls.

Following the above rules, England hit 24 fours and 2 sixes i.e. 26 boundaries and New Zealand hit 14 fours and 3 sixes i.e. 17 boundaries including the Super Over.

Accordingly, England were declared the ICC World Cup Cricket 2019 champion.

41: Rare Pearls of Figures in Women's Test Cricket

- The first ever women's Test cricket was played between Australia and England in Brisbane from Friday, December 28, 1934 to Monday, December 31, 1934 (Sunday, December 30, 1934 was rest day). Australia scored 47 and 138. England made 154 and 34 for 1. England won by 9 wickets.

- Myrtle Ethel Maclagan of England took the first ever wicket in women's Test history. Precisely, while bowling in the Australian first innings, the England bowler took the first four wickets that had fallen in Test cricket—those of Hazel Pritchard (4), Ruly Monaghan (4), Nell McLarty (0) and Essie Shevill (0). MacLagan's end-of-the-innings bowling figures were 17 overs 11 maidens 10 runs 7 wickets—the first ever instance of a bowler taking five or more wickets in a Test innings.

- In the first ever women's Test, after destroying the Australian innings with 7 wickets for 10 runs, Myrtle Ethel Maclagan of England came to open the innings for England and scored 72 runs—the first ever half-century in women's Test history. Australia's Anne Palmer took seven English wickets for 18 runs—the second instance of a bowler taking five or more wickets in a Test innings.

- In the second women's Test match in Sydney against Australia on January 7, 1935, England's Myrtle Maclagan became the first batter to register a hundred (119). With Betty Snowball (71), Maclagan added 145 runs for the first wicket, the first ever century partnership in women's Test Cricket.

Myrtle Ethel Maclagan

- Lorraine Hill of Australia became the first left-handed batter to score a hundred in women's Test. She made 118 runs not out against New Zealand in Wellington on March 23, 1975—the 46th match in women's Test annals.

- Kirsty Elizabeth Flavell (nee' Bond) (204) of New Zealand was the first double century-maker in a women's Test vs. England at Scarborough on June 27, 1996—women's Test match no. 103.

- Joanne Broadbent (200) of Australia recorded the first ever double century in women's Test by a left-handed batter—vs. England at Guildford on August 9, 1998—women's Test match no. 107.

- In women's Test cricket, the lowest score that no batter has ever made till date (dismissed or not out) is 91. No batter has ever been dismissed for 92 till date. Deborah Lea Wilson of Australia is the only batter to date to remain not out on 92—against New Zealand in Auckland on January 19, 1990. In the said innings, she came to bat at number 9 in the batting order and added 181 runs for the 8th wicket (from 157-7 to 338-8) with Sally Griffiths (133)—the world record for the 8th wicket in women's Test.

- Gargi Banerji of India holds the world record of scoring most runs in a career without a hundred in women's Tests: 614 runs in 22 innings of 12 Tests. Highest 75. Fifties 6.

- Gargi Banerji holds the Indian record of playing most innings in a career without a duck - 22 innings in 12 Tests. Her lowest score is two (made only once). In fact, she was dismissed on a single digit score in her career only five times. The world record, in this regard, is held by Charlotte Marie Edwards of England—43 innings without a duck in her career (23 Tests).

- Till date, only five batters have fallen victim to naughty 99 in women's Test cricket. (1) E. A. Snowball (England) vs. Australia at The Oval on July 13, 1937 (Snowball was run out), (2) Jill Kennare (Australia) vs. India in Mumbai on February 12, 1984, (3) Jessica Louise Jonassen (Australia) (the only left-handed to be in the 99-club) vs. England in Canterbury on August 12, 2015, (4) Ellyse Perry (Australia) vs. England in Nottingham on June 22, 2023 and (5) A J Healy (Australia) vs. South Africa in Perth on February 15, 2024.

- Till date, there have been four partnerships of 99 runs in women's Test cricket, (1) 99 runs for the 9th wicket between Suzanne Kitson (35) and Janet Tedstone (55 not out) for England against New Zealand in Auckland on January 12, 1992, (2) 99 runs for the 2nd wicket between Anju Jain (110) and Anjum Chopra (27) for India against England in Kolkata on November 20, 1995 (this match was the 99th one in women's Test history), (3) 99 runs for the 4th wicket between Sarah Elliott (104) and Alexandra Joy Blackwell (54) for Australia against England at Wormsley on August 12, 2013 and (4) 99 runs for the 1st wicket between Bethany Louise Mooney (85) and Phoebe Litchfield (46) for Australia against England in Nottingham on June 25, 2023.

- Punam Raut of India registered the 100th hundred in the history of women's Test cricket. She scored 130 off 355 balls in 426 minutes with 18 fours against South Africa in Mysore on November 16, 2014 (Test match no. 137). Raut reached century in 347 minutes off 292 balls. Her teammate Thirush Kamini scored century in the same innings only 14 minutes before Raut, off 293 balls in 348 minutes. Thus, Kamini recorded the ninety-ninth century in women's Test cricket. At the end of the first day's play, both Thirush Kamini and Punam Raut remained not out on 100. Kamini ultimately made 192.

- In women's Test cricket, the highest first innings score by a team after being sent in to bat first by the toss-winning captain is 426–7 declared off 166 overs by Pakistan against West Indies in Karachi on March 16, 2004. In this regard, the second highest score is 377–8 declared off 145 overs by India against Australia in Carrara, Queensland on October 2, 2021.

- In women's Test cricket, the world record of conceding the most runs in career by a bowler is 1647 runs in 19 Tests by Shubhangi Kulkarni of India. She took 60 wickets in her Test career. The second place also goes to an Indian—Diana Edulji. She conceded 1624 runs in 20 Tests and took 63 wickets.

- The world record of conceding most runs by a bowler in an innings in women's Test cricket is held by Shaiza Khan of Pakistan against West Indies in Karachi on March 18, 2004. In the 2nd innings of West Indies, Shaiza's bowling figures were: 55 overs 11 maidens 167 runs 6 wickets. In the West Indian first innings she took 7 wickets for 59 runs. In all, she conceded 226 runs in that match off 71 overs, another world record of conceding most runs by a bowler in both innings of a Test. Shazia's 13 wickets in this match is also a world record of most wickets in a Test.

- Diana Edulji of India holds the world record of bowling most balls in a Test career: 5098 balls in 20 Tests.

- Eight wickets for 53 runs in an innings by Neetu David of India is the best bowling figure in a Test innings on behalf of a losing team – vs. England in Jamshedpur on November 27, 1995. India (263 and 125) lost to England (196 and194) by 2 runs. In fact, along with Ashleigh Katherine Gardner of Australia (8 wickets for 66 vs. England in Nottingham

Neetu David

on June 26, 2023) and Sneh Rana of India (8 wickets for 77 vs. South Africa in Chennai on June 30, 2024), David holds the world record of taking most wickets in a Test innings by a bowler.

- A total of 149 women's Test matches have been played till August 5, 2024. Only twelve Tests have been played since December, 2014.

42: Cricket in Olympics

From April 15, 1900 to November 12, 1900 Exposition Universelle (World Fair) was held in Paris. Sports and Games were also part of this international fair. It was reported that 1226 competitors in 19 different sports participated in the Games. The duration of the sports competitions was from May 14, 1900 to October 28, 1900. As the Games were not governed by any Olympic organising body, the athletes did not have any idea that they were taking part in an Olympic event.

Cricket was included in the Exposition Universelle. Initially, Great Britain, France, Belgium and the Netherlands decided to participate, but later Belgium and the Netherlands withdrew. So, Great Britain and France were left to play the only cricket match in Olympic history.

The teams of Great Britain and France were not selected by their governing bodies of cricket. Great Britain were represented by Devon and Somerset Wanderers Club. The players of the France team belonged to French Athletic Club Union and were the British expatriates living in Paris.

It was a two-day, twelve-a-side match held on August 19–20, 1900 (Sunday and Monday) at the Velodrome de Vincennes.

Teams:

Great Britain: C.B.K. Beachcroft (Captain), Arthur Birkett, Alfred Bowerman, George Buckley, Francis Burchell, Frederick Christian, Harry Corner, Frederick Cuming, William Donne, Alfred Powlesland, John Symes, and Montagu Toller.

France: Philip Tomalin (Captain), William Anderson, William Attrill, John Braid, W. Browning, Robert Horne, Timothee Jordan, Arthur MacEvoy, Douglas Robinson, H.F. Roques, Arthur Schneidau and Henry Terry.

The match started at 11–00 a.m. on August 19, 1900. Great Britain batted first and were all out for 117. Frederick Cuming was the top scorer with 38 runs. Captain and opener Beachcroft made 23. William Anderson took 4 wickets for the French side.

In reply, France were shot out for 78 runs in their first innings. Five batters could not open their accounts. Their number 12 batter John Braid was the highest scorer with 25 (run out). Frederick Christian with seven wickets was the destroyer-in-chief for the English side. Although the French innings total was officially accepted as 78, the total of the individual scores and 11 extras shown on the scoreboard amounted to 76 only. However, no authentic clarification on this anomaly is available on record.

The second day of the match started with the beginning of the second innings of Great Britain. Alfred Bowerman (59) and captain Beachcroft (54) hit fifties. Great Britain declared their second innings at 145-5 with a lead of 184 runs. H.F. Roques of France claimed three out of five British wickets.

For France, 185 was a massive target. The French team simply collapsed in their second attempt. They lost their tenth wicket for just 11 runs. The 11th wicket stand between captain Philip Tomalin (6 not out) and John Braid (7), the top scorer in the first innings, provided a slight resistance and put on 15 runs. Twenty-six runs were all that they could garner. Six men were dismissed for duck. Montagu Toller of Great Britain became the wrecker-in-chief with 7 wickets for 9 runs.

Great Britain won the match by 158 runs just 5 minutes before the scheduled close of play. They were awarded silver medal. France were given the bronze. Later, the medals were upgraded to gold and silver respectively.

The match was officially accepted as an Olympic event only in 1912.

43: A Trilogy of Tragic 99s

Not once, but twice he was dismissed on 99. On another occasion, he ran out of his partners and remained not out on 99. His unbeaten 99 and one of the two dismissed innings of 99 came in successive Tests in a span of three innings.

The unfortunate batter on whom the three tragic 99s befell was Misbah-ul-Haq of Pakistan and on all three occasions he was captaining the side.

First 99

Misbah-ul-Haq's first 99 came in the 39th innings of his 23rd Test against New Zealand in Wellington on January 17, 2011. He came to bat at number 5 after the fall of Azhar Ali's wicket in the Pakistani first innings. The score was 144-3. Earlier, New Zealand in their first innings made 356.

Misbah added 142 runs for the fourth wicket with Younis Khan. When Pakistan lost their seventh wicket at 333, Umar Gul, the Pakistani pacer, joined him. The Pak captain was on 89. He hit a four in the last ball of the over to reach 93. The next two overs of Chris Martin and Daniel Vettori produced one run each for Misbah-ul-Haq. The second ball of Martin's 29th over was the 200th one for Misbah. He celebrated it with a delightful four through square leg and marched to 99. Pakistan 352 for 7. Misbah played out the next four balls of the over.

Pakistan increased the score by 8 runs in the next over of Vettori as Umar Gul hit a couple of fours. Misbah allowed the first ball of Martin's 30th over to go through to the wicketkeeper. The second one was played straight to the cover fielder. Misbah left his crease in search of a run that did not exist. The non-striker sent him back. Misbah's patience was wearing out. The next ball was a breakback from Martin. Misbah-ul-Haq shuffled across and attempted a flick off his leg on the off stump and missed. Out came an uproarious request from the bowler. The umpire thought a second and raised his finger. Misbah-ul-Haq lbw bowled Chris Martin 99 (310 minutes, 207 balls, 16 fours). Chronologically, it was the 83rd innings of 99 (78 times dismissed and 5 times unbeaten) in the history of Test cricket and the 10th by a Pakistani (all ten dismissed innings).

New Zealand set a target of 274 runs in the fourth innings for Pakistan's victory off a minimum of 90 overs. But before the start of the last day's play, a hole in the ground was detected. It caused a delayed start by 30 minutes and played some role in marring the possibility of Pakistan seriously chasing the target. Misbah adopted a defensive approach as they were already 1–0 up in the series. At the end of the drawn match, Misbah-ul-Haq remained not out for 70, thus missing a possible hundred which he missed so narrowly in the first innings.

Second 99

It was the antepenultimate Test match for Misbah-ul-Haq (vs. West Indies in Kingston in April, 2017), the 127th innings of his 73rd Test.

In response to West Indies' first innings of 286 runs, Misbah-ul-Haq came at number 5 at the fall of Pakistan's third wicket at 185. Batters came and left. But the captain stood his ground. At 373, Pakistan lost their 9th wicket. Mohammad Abbas, the last man, came in. Misbah was not out 68 off 180 balls at that point of time. In the next over of Gabriel, he hit a couple of fours and a couple. A huge six off the Caribbean leg-break bowler Devendra Bishoo made the captain reach 85. Another six off Bishoo's next over helped Pakistan cross 400 and Misbah reach 93. A couple of dry overs followed. The last ball of the 138th over of the innings and the 33rd over of Bishoo was delicately placed by Misbah for two. Pakistan 407–9, Misbah-ul-Haq batting 99. Mohammad Abbas, who by then faced 17 balls for his one run, had to face the full over from the right-arm off-spinner

Roston Chase. Abbas blocked the first three balls. Misbah was watching with heart in his mouth from the other end. The fourth one turned back. Abbas was beaten by the flight and went back to a full-length delivery. The turn found the ball wrapping the back foot of the batter. A boisterous chorus, formally called 'appeal,' followed and Richard Illingworth, the umpire, permitted the fall of the tenth wicket. Even before Mohammad Abbas realized what happened, Misbah-ul-Haq forced a review in a desperate attempt to save his own score from another ominous 99. But the ball-tracker confirmed the umpire's decision.

Misbah-ul-Haq, frustrated to the core of his heart, left the field with 99 not out (346 minutes, 223 balls, 5 fours, 3 sixes). This was the sixth unbeaten innings of 99, the 89th ninety-nine overall and the 11th by a Pakistani (their first unbeaten 99) in Test. The date was April 24, 2017, Monday.

In their second innings, Pakistan needed only 32 runs to win. Even to achieve that, the tourists required the service of their captain as they were reduced to 24 for 3. Misbah hit two consecutive sixes off the bowling of Bishoo and conquered the Caribbeans.

Third 99

The second Test of the series was in Bridgetown. Misbah-ul-Haq's penultimate Test—the 129th innings of his 74th Test.

West Indies won the toss, batted first and made 312 in their first innings. Pakistan, in reply, ended the second day with the score 172-3. Azhar Ali batting 81, Misbah-ul-Haq batting 7.

The fateful date was May 2, 2017, Tuesday. Captain Misbah and Azhar Ali put on 98 runs for the fourth wicket. Azhar scored 105 runs and departed leaving his team at 259-4. Asad Shafiq replaced him to join his captain. They stretched the score to 315-4. A single from long on off Devendra Bishoo gave Misbah the 99th run of his innings. Asad Shafiq simply played out the remaining four balls of the over. Now it was captain to captain. Jason Holder to Misbah. Pakistan 316-4. The first ball of Holder's 21st over was slightly short of a length. Misbah missed. The umpire disapproved of the loud shout for lbw. Holder reviewed, may be more out of hope of inserting pressure on a batter who had already two 99s in his career than anything else. The review showed the height of impact was over the stumps. Misbah survived.

The next ball was again a short pitch one, outside the off stump. Misbah-ul-Haq was in a state of

Misbah-ul-Haq

confusion—to play or not to play. First, he raised his bat with a big backlift to play the ball, but at the final nanosecond decided to withdraw. However, by then, the ball received a deadly touch from the gloves holding the bat and soared to the slip cordon. The captain helplessly saw the hopeless act of Shai Hope catching the ball. Misbah-ul-Haq could not believe his luck, or the lack of it—caught Hope bowled Holder 99 (258 minutes, 201 balls, 9 fours, 2 sixes)! The second 99 within 9 days, the third of his career—an unparalleled misfortune. It was the 90th ninety-nine in Test cricket.

But the turn of misfortune was not over for Misbah. On the last day of the match, Pakistan was asked to score 188 runs in their fourth innings for victory on an unpredictable turf. Younis Khan (5) departed leaving Pakistan at 27 for 3. As usual, Misbah came at number 5 to replace Younis. All three Caribbean pacers—Shanon Gabriel, Alzari Joseph and Jason Holder were firing on all cylinders. Misbah somehow survived an over from his counterpart Holder. Non-striker Ahmed Shehzad got a single off an edge in the first ball of the next over from Gabriel. Misbah came in the firing line. The second ball found the pad of the captain and then ballooned to Hope at gully. The umpire did not agree to the appeal for lbw. The home team sought for review. It showed the ball taking a fatal edge of the skipper's bat, and went straight to the palms of Shai Hope. An eight-ball duck for the Pakistani captain!

Pakistan lost their first seven wickets for 36 runs and the last three wickets for only three runs. West Indies won the match by 106 runs.

Misbah-ul-Haq became the third batter after Pankaj Roy of India (0 and 99 vs. Australia in Delhi in 1959–60) and Mushtaq Mohammad of Pakistan (99 run out and 0 vs. England in Karachi in 1972–73, the match that saw three batters dismissed for 99) to be dismissed for a duck and ninety-nine in the same Test.

44: One Ring, Two Fighters, Two Eras

This is a tale of two fightbacks by two fighters of two different eras in the background of failure. Once in 1952 and again in 1982. The stage: Lord's, London, the Holy of the Holies. The stars were Vinoo Mankad and Kapil Dev, the two precious gifts from India to the cricket world.

Lord's Test, 1952

Indian team led by Vijay Hazare reached England for its fourth tour with the overall Test record of one win, 12 draws and 12 defeats. India's only victory came in the last Test they played before setting off for England. They defeated England by an innings margin in Chennai on February 10, 1952. India drew the series 1–1, their first drawn series in Test cricket.

Vinoo Mankad (1952)

In that Chennai Test, Vinoo Mankad, while batting, added an invaluable 60 runs for the 3rd wicket with century-maker Pankaj Roy. And then as a bowler, he claimed eight English wickets for 55 runs off 38 overs and five balls in the first innings of the tourists. It became the Indian record of most wickets in an innings by a bowler. In the second innings of England, Mankad took four wickets for 53 runs. He, thus, became the first Indian to take 10 or more wickets in a Test match.

In November, 1951, Vinoo Mankad sought assurance from the Board of Control for Cricket in India (BCCI), in writing, for his place in the Indian team for the 1952 tour of England. BCCI did not respond in his favour. Vinoo approached Haslingden Club to play in the Lancashire League during the entire summer of 1952. C.K. Nayudu, the first Indian Test captain and the then Chairman of the Selection Committee, commented on the absence of the all-rounder from the Indian team as 'not a great loss.'

In the first Test of the 1952 summer in Leeds, India suffered a spectacular collapse in both the innings and lost the match by seven wickets. Indian team management ultimately realized the irreplaceability of Vinoo Mankad in the team and immediately knocked at the door of Haslingden Club begging for his relieving. Haslingden Club obliged.

On Thursday, June 19, 1952, the second Test at Lord's commenced. Captain Hazare won the toss and opted for batting first.

Vinoo Mankad and Pankaj Roy opened for India. Given the Leeds Test collapse, Hutton, the English captain, sought early breakthrough in the Indian innings. But Lord's was a different theatre. The defence of Pankaj Roy suddenly became impenetrable. At the other end, strokes of Vinoo Mankad started flowing like a river at the high tide.

At lunch time, the scoreboard flashed India 92–0. Mankad batting 63, Roy batting 26.

India reached 100-0 within a few minutes after lunch. Who would believe that this team lost a world record four wickets for no score in the previous Test innings in Leeds?

At 106, the first wicket fell. Vinoo was spectacularly caught by Allan Watkins at short fine leg for 72. The familiar Indian collapse reappeared. They were reduced to 170–7. The only resistance came in the form of Vijay Hazare who made 69. India were all out for 235. England ended the first day with 8–0.

On the second day, Len Hutton and Reginald Simpson started dominating the Indian bowling the way India dominated the England bowling the previous day. India lost their first wicket at 106. England also lost their first wicket at 106. Vinoo Mankad, the first victim of England in the Indian first innings, took revenge—Simpson bowled Vinoo Mankad for 53. But Hutton, with a clinical 150, and Peter May, with an elegant 74, demolished the Indian hope of easy inroads into England innings. At 292, England lost May and Watkins (0) to Mankad's spin. At stumps, England were 292–5.

A cyclone named Godfrey Evans blew the Indians away on the third morning. The strokeful cyclone that overpowered the entire bowling line-up of the tourists carried Evans on the brink of the glory of scoring a century before lunch. However, he fell two runs short and was 98 not out at lunch. Ultimately, Evans was out caught and bowled Ghulam Ahmed for 104 with 16 fours. He put on 159 with Tom Graveney (73) for the sixth wicket in 135 minutes. Jim Laker (23 not out) and Fred Trueman (17) also used long handles. In the 207th over, England were all out for 537. Vinoo did a marathon run with the ball in his hand: 73 overs, 24 maidens, 196 runs, 5 wickets—a picture of stamina.

On the third day itself, Mankad bowled 31 of his 73 overs. But captain Hazare was merciless. He ordered Vinoo 'not-a-great-loss' Mankad to pad up for opening India's second innings. It is no wonder that the reward for good work is more work!

In the second innings, Pankaj Roy left early for a duck. Coming at number 3, Hemu Adhikari made only 16. India 59–2. Hazare joined Mankad, who continued his delightful stroke-play from where he left in the first innings. All of a sudden, Alec Bedsar, Fred Trueman, Roly Jenkins, and Jim Laker lost sting in their bowling. At stumps, India were 137-2. Vinoo Mankad batting 86, Vijay Hazare batting 24.

The fourth morning belonged to Vinoo Mankad. Hazare was content in defence. But runs from the blade of Vinoo continued to flood the holy maidan of Lord's. He completed his third Test century in no time and showed no sign of caution or nerve while achieving it. Vinoo's strokeful journey continued. The landmark of 150 came and went. Before this innings, Hazare's 164 not out (vs England in Delhi in November, 1951) was the highest Test innings by an Indian. With praise in his eyes, the captain, from the non-stricker's end, saw his highest innings relegated to the second highest status. Mankad marched on.

Gradually, tiredness gripped Mankad as he entered the 180s. He and Hazare added 211 runs for the 3rd wicket, jointly the highest Indian stand in Test for that wicket at that time. Then came a sharp yorker from Laker. Mankad's tired bat could not come down quickly. Mankad bowled Laker 184, a new Indian record. An epic innings of 270 minutes, studded with 19 fours and one six. Out of 133 runs that India added that day till his dismissal, contribution of Vinoo Mankad was 98.

Hazare (49) left quickly. G. Ramchand gave some resistance with 42. India were all out for 378, just 76 runs ahead.

England needed 77 runs to go 2–0 up in the series, a mere formality. Ramchand and Hazare opened the bowling in the second innings of England, but bowled only one over each. Then again, the bowling machine of Vinoo Mankad and Ghulam Ahmed rolled on. The easy task of England started to look not that easy.

Simpson (2) left at the team's score of seven. England finished the day with 40 for 1. Hutton batting 27, Peter May batting 8.

Lion-hearted Mankad and Ghulam Ahmed continued to bowl tight in the next morning. England's progress to the winning tape became slower. At 71, Ghulam Ahmed got rid of Peter May for 26. But determined Hutton and Denis Compton achieved the victory in the second ball of the 50th over. Vinoo's untiring bowling figures: 24 overs, 12 maidens, 35 runs, no wicket.

England won the match, but Mankad won the heart of the connoisseurs of cricket at its holiest shrine.

Lord's 1982

As if it was the reincarnation of Vinoo Mankad. On August 21, 1978, Mankad left this mundane world for good, and exactly 56 days later, another great all-rounder of India put his first footprint on the arena of Test cricket (vs. Pakistan in Faisalabad on October 16, 1978)—a hard-hitting batter and a fast bowling talent rolled into one. Kapil Dev Ramlal Nikhanj was born exactly 36 days before the great Vinoo Mankad played his last Test match (vs. West Indies in Delhi on February 11, 1959).

Kapil Dev (1982)

And 30 years after Vinoo's heroics, this sensational Haryana Hurricane chose the holy stage of Lord's to replicate the fighting spirit of his predecessor.

In 1982, India toured England for the 10th time to play a Test series. Like 1952, this time also England was India's opponent (at home) just before this series. At home, in 1981–82, India won the series 1–0.

First Test at Lord's started on June 10, 1982. Bob Willis, the England captain, won the toss and decided to bat first.

Ball was moving in the air more than Willis anticipated. Kapil Dev struck early. Geoff Cook (4) was plumbed lbw. Allan Lamb (9), the number three batter, was also adjudged lbw to Kapil Dev. Kapil's third victim was opener Chris Tavare (4), caught by G.R. Viswanath. He was Kapil's 150th Test victim (in 67 bowling innings of 39 Tests). England 37–3.

Gower and Botham steadied the ship. Strokes began to flow with more spontaneity and assurance. They put on 59 runs for the 4th wicket. It was again Kapil Dev who broke the stand—Gower caught Viswanath bowled Kapil Dev 37 off 83 balls with 2 fours. England 96–4.

Derek Randall returned to the England team after almost two years. He joined Botham. They added 53 for the 5th wicket before Botham fell to Madan Lal for 67 off 105 balls with 8 fours and one six.

Randall's comeback became memorable as he scored his third Test century (126 runs off 290 balls in 353 minutes with 11 fours and a six). As the pitch and weather gradually became more batting-friendly, the late-order English batters also contributed. The last wicket partnership between Paul Allott (41 not out) and Bob Willis (28) added 70 runs. England were all out for 433. Kapil Dev finished with 5 wickets for 125 runs off 43 overs.

If England, in the early part of their innings, were reduced to 37–3, can India be far behind? Captain Sunil Gavankar, as usual, started batting with safety and solidity of the Red Fort. But at the other end, Ghulam Parkar (6), whose batting ability never deserved a place in the national team, Dilip Vengsarkar (2), G.R. Viswanath (1), Yashpal Sharma (4) and Ashok Malhotra (5) made their visit to the crease very short. On a pitch that suddenly started behaving differently, India's score became 45 for 5 wickets in no time.

Kapil Dev joined Gavaskar. Spasm of life started being felt in the body of the Indian innings. Sedate Gavaskar and flamboyant Kapil doubled the score. India were 92 for 5 at the draw of stumps on the second day.

Next morning, Kapil Dev departed at the team's score of 112. His innings of 41, the second highest after Gavaskar's 48, lasted for 91 minutes and 69 balls. However, India got vanished for 128 and earned the ignominy of follow on.

In the second innings, Gavaskar (24) left early and India finished the weather-affected day with

61–2. Vengsarkar batting 30, Ravi Shastri batting 6. Only two and a half hours of play was possible.

After taking rest on Sunday, June 13, Vengsankar came to the crease fresh and alive. Three years back, he scored a match-saving hundred on this ground. Now he was in a mood to enjoy run-bath. Being tortured by the middle of his blade, ball after ball delivered by the home team bowlers raced beyond the boundary in search of peace.

Between lunch and tea, Vengsarkar garnered 86 runs. A partnership of 142 runs with Yashpal Sharma (37) for the 5th wicket strengthened the Indian reply. However, at 252, England captain dislodged both the batters. Vengsarkar made 157 in 334 minutes off 264 balls with 21 fours.

Kapil came at number seven in the first innings and registered the second highest score. That perhaps did not impress Gavaskar, his captain. This time he was sent at number eight.

Calamity broke out instantaneously. Kapil started from where Vengsarkar left. Still, India needed 53 more to avoid innings defeat. As Kapil's bat started sparkling with strokes, Indian supporters came alive for the second time in the second innings. The English crowd got a bit dismayed.

Wicketkeeper Syed Kirmani (3) left at 275. Madan Lal joined and reduced himself to the role of a spectator as Kapil went on with his act of disrespect to the English bowlers with his arrogant strokeplay. India avoided innings defeat. Kapil's fifty came off just 35 balls. He was in no mood to stop. His high strike rate put Roy Fredericks' the then fastest century off 71 balls in peril.

At 341, Madan Lal fell lbw to Derek Pringle. Kapil Dev and Madan Lal added 66 runs for the 9th wicket in 33 minutes. Madan Lal contributed only 15 runs. India were just 36 runs ahead.

Dilip Doshi, as number 11 with the then career aggregate of 99 runs in 25 Tests, joined Kapil Dev, who attempted to score runs as fluently as he did during the previous wicket stand and to protect Doshi's lack of batting skill from the opponent attack.

At 369, the resistance of Kapil Dev came to an end when the swashbuckling all-rounder was caught at short midwicket for 89, which came off just 55 balls in 77 minutes with 13 fours and 3 sixes. The last wicket added 28 runs in 17 minutes. Doshi's contribution was four singles as he crossed the hundred run mark of his career aggregate.

In 1952, England needed 77 runs for victory. In 1982, England required 65 runs for victory. At the beginning of both the innings, it looked like a mere formality to the home team. In 1952, the never-say-die approach of Vinoo Mankad and Ghulam Ahmed made the task of England tougher than they thought. In 1982, it was the turn of giant-hearted Kapil Dev.

In the fading light of the fourth evening, the Haryana Hurricane shattered the defence of Chris Tavare (1). England 11–1. A couple of runs later, nightwatchman Bob Taylor (1) waved goodbye to the playing arena. Kapil had him caught by Ashok Malhotra. Then came the turn of opener Geoff Cook (10) to fall victim to Kapil Dev. England 18–3! Followers of Indian cricket were rubbing their eyes in disbelief.

The same thing happened, or almost the same thing, one year and 124 days back in Test cricket's earliest venue Melbourne. Australia had a target of 143 runs to beat India and at the fag end of the 4th day's play, they lost John Dyson (3) and Greg Chappell (0), the captain, in successive balls off Karson Ghavri. Like at Lord's, where the opener Geoff Cook departed to make the score 18–3, in Melbourne also, opener Graeme Wood was amazingly stumped by Syed Kirmani off Dilip Doshi for 10 and Australia were 18–3. At Lord's, England ended the 4th day's play with score 23–3. In Melbourne, Australia ended the 4th day's play with score 24–3. In Melbourne, injured Kapil Dev took pain-killer, and with the help of Dilip Doshi

(22-9-33-2), pulverized the strong Aussie batting line-up for 83. Kapil took 5 for 28.

This time? Would his act of Melbourne repeat? Or, would the history of Lord's, 1952 repeat?

History of Lord's, 1952 repeated on June 15, 1982. Not the miracle of Melbourne. Kapil tried his best since the first ball of the last day. But no movement in the air, no help from the pitch, no help from the other end of the wicket. Lamb and Gower did not relax and England earned a seven-wicket victory in the 19th over. Kapil's bowling figures: 10 overs, 1 maiden, 43 runs, 3 wickets.

Kapil Dev became the Player of the Match. But his soul remained sad and unsatiated, as was the case of Vinoo Mankad, 30 years back.

One year and ten days later. The stage was again Lord's. Occasion: World Cup Final. Saturday, June 25, 1983. Captain Kapil Dev lifted the World Cup. The unfinished miracle of June 15, 1982 at last found an emotional and memorable end. Invincible West Indies of Clive Lloyd were conquered by Kapil's devils. India became the world champion coming from nowhere.

Cricket is the greatest snatcher. Cricket is the greatest donor too.

45: Nottingham Sunset, Nottingham Sunrise

The stage was set for a memorable occasion for the connoisseurs and chroniclers of cricket. The first ever 5-Test rubber was going to be hosted by the motherland of cricket. England vs. Australia. The series would start in Nottingham, Robin Hood's own country. And it would be the first ever Test match in Nottingham—a three-day affair between June 1 and June 3, 1899 (Thursday-Saturday).

W.G. Grace

The Nottingham Test was the last Test of W.G. Grace of England, the first superhero of the game. At the same time, the Test match, which was chronologically the 52nd one between England and Australia, saw the Test debut of two more legends of cricket—Wilfred Rhodes of England and Victor Trumper of Australia.

Born on July 18, 1848 in Bristol, William Gilbert Grace, with the help of his all-round cricketing skills and towering personality, gradually became the father figure of the game. His first-class cricket career lasted from 1865 to 1908 and his Test career from 1880 to 1899. In first-class cricket, he amassed 54,211 runs (the fifth highest of all time) in 870 matches with 124 centuries (only ten batters scored more centuries) at an average of 39.45. As a right-arm medium pacer, Grace claimed 2809 wickets at an average of 18.14. Only nine bowlers had taken more wickets than Grace in first-class cricket. In Test cricket, he appeared 22 times for England and scored 1098 runs with two hundreds at an average of 32.29. He bagged nine Test wickets also at an average of 26.22. However, cricket remembers him more as a batter than a bowler. At the time of his retirement, his 1098 Test runs stood third in the list of the highest career aggregate after Arthur Shrewsbury (1227) of England and A.C. Bannerman (1108) of Australia. To add to it, Grace was the first batter ever to score a Test century on England soil and that too on his Test debut.

But W.G. Grace was too great a cricketer to be caged in the formality of figures. One has to remember that during the Grace era, pitch remained uncovered and a considerable portion of his remarkably strokeful innings were played on pitches which nowadays would have been declared underprepared. Bowlers bowled the balls, turns and bounces of which were beyond predictability.

There were no restrictions on bouncers, no field restrictions on the fielding side. There were no helmets, no good quality protective gear available for the batters. And despite all these, the doctor (Grace obtained LRCP and MRCP from the University of Edinburgh) gifted 54,211 runs to first-class cricket. The spontaneous expression of Ranjitsinhji, the first Indian cricketer to play Test cricket (for England vs Australia in Manchester in 1896), immortalised the contribution of W.G. as a batter to cricket. In his book 'The Jubilee Book of Cricket,' Ranji opined, "He revolutionized batting. He turned it from an accomplishment into a science... I hold him not only the finest player born or unborn, but the maker of modern batting. He turned the old one-stringed instrument into a many-chorded lyre...The theory of modern batting is in all essentials the result of W.G's thinking and working on the game."

As regards the influence of Grace as a cricketer on the era he belonged to, John Arlott, the ace commentator and writer made the emphatic statement, "Certainly no sportsman of our era has had such a profound effect on the social life of his time. He was at once a father-figure, a hero, a performer of sporting near-miracles and a well-loved human being." Sir Neville Cardus, the W.G. Grace of cricket-writing, observed, "In my home, when I was a boy, there were no cricketers, and little talk of any form of sport, but most summer mornings at breakfast the name of W.G. Grace was pronounced with that of Mr. Gladstone... The Royal Family inquired about the health of Grace from time to time. Small boys, playing primitively in fields or on the pavements of growing cities, struck defiant attitudes with their bats and said they were W.G." Sir Cardus further penned, "In those days the line between county and country cricket was slenderly drawn. Grace journeyed right and left, playing with the greatest and the humblest—now at Lord's against the Australians, now in Thornbury against the lads of the village... He played in these modest engagements with all the keenness he put into a Test match."

W.G. Grace completed his 50 years of age in 1898. Now, a year later, he was slower in fielding and running between the wickets. His bowling lost penetration. Runs were not flowing out of his bat as fluently and frequently as those were earlier.

In 1899, an independent selection committee was in place in England. Arthur Shrewsbury, one of the finest batters of Nottinghamshire and England, especially on sticky wickets, expressed his willingness to play for England. In the earlier days, when there was no selection committee and the host county authorities did the selection job, Shrewsbury would have been a certainty in the team. But now the selection committee, consisting of Lord Hawke, W.G. Grace himself, Herbert Bainbridge, F.S. Jackson and C.B. Fry, did not select Shrewsbury. On the other hand, three of the five selectors (Grace, Jackson and Fry) included themselves in the England team. All these factors determined the mood of the local cricket fans right before the start of the Test in Nottingham.

On the first day of the Nottingham Test, Australian captain Joe Darling won the toss and chose to bat first. W.G. bowled twenty-five five-ball overs without success. Australia's first innings ended at 252. Grace and Fry opened the England innings and added 75 runs for the first wicket. Amidst jeering, Grace struggled to reach 28 and was out. While fielding in the second innings, people made a loud noise of disapproval when Grace dropped Clem Hill in the early part of his innings. Ultimately, the doctor took a smart catch to dismiss Hill, but by that time Hill earned 80 valuable runs for Australia. In England's second innings, Grace could score only one run. By then, the bearded doctor decided to make this Test his swansong.

The Sun went down behind the river Trent forever.

***

The batton of greatness was passed from one generation to the next. The setting of one Sun heralded the rise of another.

Wilfred Rhodes, the 121st Test cricketer of England, made his Test debut in Nottingham on June 1, 1899 at the age of 21 years 215 days. And his Test career went on and on and on till the washout of the 9th day's play on April 12, 1930 against West Indies in Kingston. He was 52-year-165-day old by then, the oldest Test cricketer ever, breaking the world record of 50 years 320 days owned by W.G. Grace! And Rhodes' Test career of 30 years 315 days continues to remain a world record as the longest Test career.

Wilfred Rhodes

Rhodes is only the second player in Test history to bat at every position from number 1 to number 11 after Sydney Edward Gregory of Australia. He is the only batter in Test cricket to hold the world record for the first wicket partnership and the world record for the last wicket partnership simultaneously for 38 years 291 days. He also held the world record of the highest partnership for any wicket (323 runs for the first wicket with Jack Hobbs) for 22 years 161 days.

In first-class cricket, Wilfred Rhodes scored 39,969 runs (the 17th highest) in 1534 innings (the world record of most innings played) of 1110 matches (the world record of most matches played). As a bowler, he continues to hold the world record of the most wickets—4204 wickets off world record number of 1,85,742 balls. He claimed at least five wickets in an innings 287 times, the second highest ever after Alfred Percy Freeman of Kent and England (386 times in 592 matches) and ten wickets in a match 68 times (the sixth highest in the all time list). In 58 Tests, Rhodes scored 2325 runs with two centuries (179 and 152) and 11 fifties at an average of 30.19 and bagged 127 wickets (Best bowling: 8 wickets for 68) at an average of 26.96. The statistical achievements of Wilfred Rhodes know no end.

Rhodes started his career mainly as a bowler, a left-arm orthodox spinner. Gradually, without sacrificing his bowling skills, he started enhancing his batting ability. Sir Neville Cardus was so impressed by his all-round ability that once, while attempting to select a World XI, he remarked, “I am prepared to go to any extreme of subterfuge and sophistry to get Wilfred into my World XI.” While analysing his bowling, the great poet of cricket composed, "Rhodes gets his men out before the ball pitches; spin with him is an accessory after the act of flight—flight which disguises the ball's length, draws the batsman forward when he ought to play back, sends him playing back when he ought to come forward, and generally keeps him in a state of mind so confused that in time he begins to feel it might be a mercy to get out."

Coming back to his debut Test, captain Grace threw the ball to Rhodes to deliver the first ball of the match. In the Australian first innings, he bowled 35 overs and 2 balls and took the wickets of in-form Monty Noble (41), debutant F. Laver (3), W.P. Howell (0) and Earnie Jones (4) for 58 runs. In the second innings, the debutant bowler dismissed the opener and captain Joe Darling (14), Monty Noble (45) and Hugh Trumble (38) for 60 runs off 20 five-ball overs. In the only innings he batted in this Test, Rhodes came at number 10 and scored six runs.

The comment of his Yorkshire senior teammate George Hurbert Hirst to Rhodes in the 5th Test at The Oval in 1902 against Australia is now a part of the cricket lore, "Wilfred, we'll get these runs in singles." England who trailed by 141 runs in the first innings to Australia, were in need of 263 runs for victory. They lost their first five wickets for 48 runs. Further slide was arrested when G.L. Jessop launched a fierce counter-attack and reached century in the then world record time of 75 minutes. Stanley Jackson made 49 runs. And still, when England lost their 9th wicket, they were 15 short of touching the harbour of victory. The last man in was Wilfred Rhodes, whose career aggregate up to the first innings of this Test was just 79 runs in 10 innings. Then came the proposal from Hirst. To quote from Bill Frindall's 'The Wisden Book of Test Cricket' (Volume I), "Hirst and Rhodes calmly acquired the 15 runs needed for victory (not all in singles) during one of cricket's most historic last-wicket partnerships." To some chroniclers, this little innings of Rhodes injected a decisive ounce of inspiration inside him and led to considerable improvement in his batting skill. The rest is history.

***

The second Sun that rose on the eastern horizon of Nottingham in that summer of 1899 was a batting artist from Darlinghurst, Sydney. He was junior to Wilfred Rhodes by five days in terms of age. Victor Thomas Trumper is chronologically the 79th cricketer to play Test for Australia. He was the fifth batter in Test History to score double century and only the second to Clem Hill, his compatriot, to garner 2000 and 3000 runs in Test career. Overall, he played 48 Tests and registered 3163 runs at an average of 39.04 with eight hundred-plus innings. In first-class cricket,

Trumper's kitty held 16,939 runs in 255 matches with 42 centuries at an average of 44.57. He was the first batter in Test cricket to reach century before lunch on the first day (vs. England in Manchester in 1902).

Like all other greats of the game, the genius of Trumper could not be measured with the tapes of runs and centuries. He inhaled cricket since his childhood. At the age of 17, he fabricated a delightful innings of 67 against A.E. Stoddart's visiting English team. This innings paved the way to his selection in the state team of New South Wales. From then on, there was no looking back for Trumper. He played his first Test in Nottingham in 1899.

Victor Trumper

In the Nottingham Test in 1899, Trumper's team batted first. Australia were packed with stars like captain Darling, Monty Noble, Clem Hill, Syd Gregory and Frank Iredale. At 166, Australia lost their 4th wicket. Trumper arrived at the crease as number 6. Hill, his partner, took a single off Jack Hearne, the Middlesex and England medium pacer. But Trumper did not last long. He was bowled by Hearne for no score. What a valueless start to an invaluable career! In the second innings, Stanley Jackson knocked off his stumps for 11.

England were asked to make 290 runs in the 4th innings for victory. At one time, they were 19 for the loss of W.G. (1), Jackson (0), Gunn (3) and Fry (9). But the fighting brilliance of Trumper's clone in terms of style, Ranjitsinhji (93 not out) and T.W. Hayward (28) saved the day for England (155 for 7).

The Nottingham Test ended in a draw, but became a witness to one nostalgic sunset and two promising sunrises.

The beauty of batting bloomed to the full in the blade of Trumper in the second Test at Lord's. In response to England's first innings of 206, Australia lost Jack Worrall (18), Joe Darling (9) and Syd Gregory (15) for 59 runs. Clem Hill and Monty Noble (54) staged a recovery with a partnership of 130 runs for the 4th wicket and brought Australia within 17 runs of England's first innings total. Rhodes dislodged Noble. Trumper came at number 6 and added 82 runs for the 5th wicket with Clem Hill, who made 135. With Hugh Trumble (24), Trumper added 80 runs for the 7th wicket. Ultimately, Australia were all out for 421. Trumper remained unconquered till the end. After Trumper's arrival at the wicket, Australia put on 232 runs. Trumper's contribution was 135.

This innings of 135 not out by Victor Trumper was a statement to the connoisseurs of world cricket—an innings that blended serene beauty and graceful audacity together in stroke-making. His show of brilliance lasted for 195 minutes and was beautified with 20 fours.

After the innings was over, the bearded, big-hearted legend from Gloucestershire, who already sang the tune of sayonara in the previous Test in Nottingham, came to Trumper and presented him with a bat inscribed "From the past champion to the future champion." The old eyes of W.G. never failed to succeed in detecting the sparkles on the oval ground.

About the Author

Sekhar Ranjan Amin has retired as Director from Department of Posts with a total experience of over 35 years across ministries like Department of Commerce, Ministry of Defence, Ministry of Environment, Forest and Climate Change etc.

Since his college days, Sekhar has taken writing on sports seriously and has contributed a number of articles, especially on cricket, in the regional periodicals.

He is an M.A. in Journalism from the Calcutta University with Sports Journalism as a special paper. At a very young age he excelled in the world of quiz and won a number of quiz competitions. When he was 21, he utilised the opportunity of showcasing his skill as a cricket statistician in a book (in Bengali) on cricket laws named 'Cricketer Umpire' written by renowned Test umpire Samar Roy.

Beyond the world of writing, Sekhar is an intense mountain-lover. In his younger days, he travelled from corner to corner in the Himalayas-Karakoram mountain ranges to explore the life and style of the villages and hamlets there and to enjoy the flora and fauna and the mystic beauty of the non-living nature.

Now, as he has retired from service, Sekhar has taken up pen to write down his first book "Sparkles On The Oval Ground."

Image Sources:

Chapter 1 -

https://www.indiatoday.in/education-today/gk-current-affairs/story/vijay-hazare-312785-2016-03-11

Chapter 3 -

https://oldebor.wordpress.com/2022/09/14/like-the-crack-of-doom-the-emergence-of-amar-singh/

Chapter 4 -

https://www.thecricketpaper.com/features/featured/3157/when-don-bradman-and-the-oval-witnessed-the-south-london-grounds-best-delivery/

chapter 5 -

https://en.wikipedia.org/wiki/Phiroze_Palia

https://www.cricketcountry.com/news/vinod-kambli-retires-from-first-class-cricket-5848/

Chapter 6 -

https://www.espncricinfo.com/cricketers/bhagwath-chandrasekhar-27591/photos

Chapter 8 -

https://en.wikipedia.org/wiki/Walter_Read

Chapter 9 -

https://www.indiatoday.in/sports/cricket/story/shane-warne-dies-muttiah-muralitharan-tribute-legendary-spinners-1920884-2022-03-04

Chapter 10 -

https://tribune.com.pk/article/51300/remembering-mushtaq-mohammad-the-legendary-epitome-of-pakistan-cricket-captaincy

https://www.cricket.com/news/first-hundreds-scored-all-across-formats-1660245634822

https://www.scoreline.org/majid-khan-the-el-magnifico/

Chapter 11 -

https://en.wikipedia.org/wiki/Charles_Bannerman

https://www.cricketcountry.com/articles/lala-amarnath-21-curious-facts-about-indias-first-test-centurion-185776/

Chapter 12 -

https://timesofindia.indiatimes.com/city/kolkata/who-is-bina-das/articleshow/67689539.cms

https://www.theguardian.com/sport/2020/may/26/stanley-jackson-batting-master-mp-sportsman-bewitched-cardus-cricket-the-spin

Chapter 14 -

https://www.indiatoday.in/sports/cricket/story/ck-nayudu-birth-anniversary-1379200-2018-10-31

https://www.crictracker.com/i-wasnt-even-half-good-without-the-support-of-seniors-kapil-dev-praises-1983-world-cup-winning-team/

Chapter 15 -

https://www.indiatvnews.com/sports/cricket/amazing-facts-about-the-legend-brian-lara-who-turned-45-11636.html

Chapter 16 -

https://www.zapcricket.com/blogs/newsroom/the-universe-boss-chris-gayle

Chapter 17 -

https://www.thecricketer.com/Topics/wc2019_player_profiles/hazratullah_zazai.html

Chapter 18 -

https://www.mediastorehouse.co.uk/topfoto/1920s/sport/charles-albert-george-jack-russell-essex-county-11015704.html

Chapter 19 -

https://en.wikipedia.org/wiki/James_Southerton

Chapter 20 -

https://en.wikipedia.org/wiki/Hanif_Mohammad

Chapter 22 -

https://www.aajtak.in/sports/cricket/photo/on-this-day-jim-laker-takes-all-ten-wickets-in-one-innings-england-vs-australia-manchester-test-match-1956-tspo-1747218-2023-07-31-1

Chapter 24 -

https://simple.wikipedia.org/wiki/Don_Bradman

Chapter 26 -

https://en.wikipedia.org/wiki/Vijay_Merchant

Chapter 29 -

https://www.theguardian.com/sport/blog/2012/dec/30/tony-greig-cricket-great

https://www.onmanorama.com/sports/vantage-point/2020/04/19/alvin-kallicharran-west-indies-india-wsc-rebel-tour.html

Chapter 30 -

https://www.espncricinfo.com/cricketers/mudassar-nazar-41308/photos

https://www.livemint.com/sports/cricket-news/death-of-test-cricket-australias-steve-waugh-warns-icc-bcci-says-can-t-allow-profits-to-define-legacy-11704187144571.html

Chapter 31 -

https://www.telegraph.co.uk/cricket/2022/05/02/wisden-trims-wg-graces-first-class-record-two-hundreds-685-runs/

Chapter 32 -

https://en.wikipedia.org/wiki/Billy_Murdoch

Chapter 33 -

https://en.wikipedia.org/wiki/Warwick_Armstrong

https://en.wikipedia.org/wiki/Alex_Moir

Chapter 35-

https://www.rnz.co.nz/news/sport/327714/lee-germon-from-canterbury-to-sydney

Chapter 36 -

https://www.espncricinfo.com/cricketers/gordon-greenidge-51901/photos

Chapter 38 -

https://indianexpress.com/article/sports/cricket/im-heading-to-the-ipl-brian-lara-blames

-franchise-cricket-for-decline-of-test-cricket-in-west-indies-9111071/

https://en.wikipedia.org/wiki/Bob_Simpson_%28cricketer%29

Chapter 39 -

https://sportstar.thehindu.com/cricket/mahela-jayawardene-cricket-sri-lanka-sports-indian-cricket-team-news/article31545997.ece

https://sports.ndtv.com/icc-cricket-world-cup-2015/kumar-sangakkara-craves-for-records-despite-creaking-joints-1503798

Chapter 40 -

https://www.livemint.com/sports/cricket-news/ipl-2024-nobody-would-have-bought-ben-stokes-aakash-chopra-gives-his-two-cents-about-csk-releasing-england-cricketer-11701058071219.html

https://www.newsbytesapp.com/news/sports/presenting-new-zealand-pacer-trent-boult-s-odi-career-in-numbers/story

Chapter 41 -

https://en.wikipedia.org/wiki/Myrtle_Maclagan

https://timesofindia.indiatimes.com/sports/cricket/news/bcci-appoints-neetu-david-as

-head-of-womens-selection-panel/articleshow/78334994.cms

Chapter 43 -

https://sports.ndtv.com/cricket/misbah-ul-haq-will-remain-pakistan-test-captain-if-he-keeps-playing-1659466

Chapter 44 -

https://www.thequint.com/sports/cricket/vinoo-mankad-unknown-facts

https://www.indiatoday.in/sports/story/kapil-dev-was-a-man-of-few-words-he-was-a-man-of-action-302375-2016-01-06

Chapter 45 -

https://www.telegraph.co.uk/cricket/2022/05/02/wisden-trims-wg-graces-first-class-record-two-hundreds-685-runs/

https://en.wikipedia.org/wiki/Wilfred_Rhodes

https://www.cricketcountry.com/articles/victor-trumper-the-batsman-often-rated-above-don-bradman-19278/